"Nancy Mujo Baker's new book, *Opening to Oneness,* is subtitled 'A Practical and Philosophical Guide to the Zen Precepts.' She could well have added the word *Compassionate.* While her philosophical inquiry is deep and wide-ranging, it's her emphasis on bringing a nonjudgmental and accepting yet brave and probing spirit to the whole of life that makes this presentation of the Buddhist precepts so refreshing and inspiring.

"Her intimacy with Dogen's teachings on the simultaneity of oneness and particularity infuses every aspect of the book. She works with each of the precepts as a koan, asking us to bring awareness to the uncertainty and discomfort that come forth when we do so. Phrasing each precept as a gerund—non-killing, non-blaming—rather than as a dualistic commandment, she returns us to ourselves, in all our messy wholeness. When we courageously face the conditions that bring about suffering, she attests, we can awaken to the truth that we are not separate from anyone or anything.

"This is a book that does indeed offer a practical guide but also always pushes us to go further. Leaping out from the confines of conceptual thinking, we can leap into the experience of faith that makes Zen practice so transformative."

—Shinge Roko Sherry Chayat, coeditor of *Eloquent Silence* and *Endless Vow*

"This is an exceptional guide through the precepts, illuminating them in ways that bring them to life in our daily living. The author is not only a long-time Zen adept, deeply conversant with Dogen, but also a major league philosophy professor in addition to having studied for twenty years in the Diamond Approach, all of which allow her to shine the light of several perspectives on these critical aspects of our life. She also happens to be a marvelous writer, allowing the reader to feel that they're in the hands of a true master of thought, word, and deed, as well as insight, practice, and wisdom. It has been a long time in the making, and it feels like a grace to encounter this scintillating and galvanizing work."

—Henry Shukman, author of *One Blade of Grass: Finding the Old Road of the Heart—A Zen Memoir*

"A fascinating and informative discussion, along with recommendations for group exercises, explicating the dictum that there is 'no Buddhism without precepts.' The section on Dogen's approach based on unifying in all possible ways with these aspects of life experience is especially illuminating."

—Steven Heine, author of *Dogen: Japan's Original Zen Teacher*

"What a wonderful book. It is Nancy Baker's gift to translate the Buddhist precepts in such a way that they become fruitful and inspiring for every person who seeks in their spiritual path for skillful means in their daily life. She offers in the second part of the book a bright view into Zen teachings, especially for Westerners."

—Anna Myoan Gamma, founder of Zen Zentrum Offener Kreis

"This is the guide we have always needed! Nancy Mujo Baker's lucid and intimate companion to the moral and ethical teachings of Zen offers us two dimensions: a deeply personal guide to our own individual resources for living an ethical life, including personal exercises, and also, by virtue of her years teaching philosophy, a superbly understandable exploration of the Buddhist principles of the nondual, of suchness, of true compassion. Bringing these elements together, using ordinary examples of complex ideas, Baker offers the first truly coherent study of Zen precepts. I love it!"

—Pat Enkyo O'Hara, author of *Most Intimate: A Zen Approach to Life's Challenges*

"This wise and brave book on the precepts is an extraordinary resource and source of inspiration about what it means to meet the world with integrity and strength. I wholeheartedly recommend it to all who want to realize a life of care, compassion, and engagement with the truth of suffering and freedom from suffering. This is the guidebook par excellence that reveals the path to oneness."

—Joan Halifax, author of *Being with Dying* and *Standing at the Edge*

"Zen teacher Mujo Baker deftly wields her wisdom sword, finely honed through years of a rigorous spiritual journey, to help us plunge into an exploration and experience of Oneness. Using the Zen Buddhist precepts as her focus, she provides a clear and simple method to open to the parts of oneself that are instinctively suppressed and which, therefore, often lead one to oppressing others. The reader might also find themself transformed by Mujo's engaging and succinct discourses on Oneness, nonduality, and non-separation. This book is an excellent contribution to the Zen precept literature. I highly recommend it to those who aspire to live fully their very best life."

—Wendy Egyoku Nakao, co-author of
The Book of Householder Koans: Waking Up in the Land of Attachments

"Roshi Nancy Baker invokes Japanese Zen Master Dogen and sheds fresh light on the Buddhist precepts—not as a list of 'shoulds and should nots,' but as a way of awakened living, a way of opening to Oneness in all the dimensions of our lives."

—Ruben L.F. Habito, author of
Be Still and Know: Zen and the Bible

Opening to Oneness

Opening to Oneness

A Practical and Philosophical Guide to the Zen Precepts

NANCY MUJO BAKER

SHAMBHALA

Shambhala Publications, Inc.
2129 13th Street
Boulder, Colorado 80302
www.shambhala.com

Cover art: "Leaping Carp" by Ohara Koson, Robert O. Muller Collection
Cover design: Daniel Urban-Brown
Interior design: Gopa & Ted2, Inc.

9 8 7 6 5 4 3 2 1

First Edition
Printed in the United States of America
♻ Shambhala Publications makes every effort to print on acid-free, recycled paper.
Shambhala Publications is distributed worldwide by Penguin Random House, Inc., and its subsidiaries.

Page 248 constitutes a continuation of the copyright page.

In memory of
Bernard Tetsugen Glassman Roshi,
"Bernie,"
my first and only Zen teacher

Followers of the Way, the Dharma of the Mind has no form and pervades the Ten Directions. In the eye it is called seeing; in the ear, hearing; in the nose, smelling; in the feet, walking. . . . If you want to get free from birth and death, from coming and going, from taking and putting on, know and take hold of him who is now listening to the Dharma. He has neither form nor shape, neither root nor trunk; nor does he have a dwelling place; he is as lively as fish jumping in water and performs his function in response to all situations. Only, the place of functioning is not a locality.

MASTER RINZAI (CH. LINJI)

Contents

Acknowledgments

FIRST, THANKS goes to my Zen teacher of forty years, my original teacher, Roshi Bernie Glassman. I am indebted to him in so many ways for the depth of his teaching, but also for empowering me, as a lay teacher, to be a preceptor. This has meant giving the precepts in the Jukai ceremony, which has taught me more than I can say about the Zen precepts. I thank him also for encouraging me many years ago to work in groups and to appreciate the value of what we called then "befriending the self" in preparation for discovering that it is not what we think it is.

As many Zen practitioners know, the center of Bernie's work was in the social action sphere where not knowing, bearing witness, and loving action—the Three Tenets he developed for the Zen Peacemaker Order—are used as guides for practice in this "outer world." Although I was with him in Yonkers when he began all his remarkable social action work, I did not follow him in this. Instead, in addition to leaning more toward the wisdom aspect of Zen, the foundations of which I totally owe to him, I remained a full-time academic philosopher with a great interest in the transformation of the individual. What is striking is how much I have remained his student. We both developed a strong interest in what we might call "rejected or split off parts." He was interested in the split-off parts of the social world; I was and remain interested in what has been split-off in the personal and philosophical worlds. I might say that, in my case, something like the Three Tenets have been used as guides for practice in the inner world and surprisingly even for reading and understanding Wittgenstein, my academic specialty. Ultimately, of course, there is no difference between the inner and the outer. Bernie's death has been a great loss to all of us.

Second, thanks goes to Hameed Ali (A. H. Almaas), whose Diamond Approach has taught me over a period of twenty years that true liberation requires a deep and careful transformation of *all* aspects of what it is to be a human being. In addition to that, I have the deepest gratitude to him for having taken me on as a private student, a truly priceless gift that has allowed me to articulate and understand the depths of my own experience, something often discouraged in Zen. Third, thanks go to all those students of the No Traces Sangha who have worked so deeply on the precepts in the yearlong preparations for the Jukai ceremony, and from whom I have learned a great deal. Special thanks goes to Adam Feder, whose practical help and enthusiastic support when my own enthusiasm was flagging have been invaluable. Thanks also goes to Roshi Ray Cicetti, resident teacher of the Empty Bowl Zendo and dharma heir of Roshi Robert Kennedy. He and I went through a precept study together in preparation for his Jukai ceremony, and again in preparation for the preceptor ceremony, which empowered him to give the precepts. It was a privilege to do this with a fellow teacher in the White Plum lineage of Hakuyu Taizan Maezumi Roshi.

Fourth, and perhaps most importantly, I want to thank *Tricycle* magazine for having initiated the publication, one at a time, of these essays on the precepts, which were originally dharma talks. The writing of this book would not have happened without the deadlines and small monthly bits of editing that resulted in the written version of the original talks on each of the precepts.

Last of all, but by no means least, I'd like to thank Hee-Jin Kim for his three splendid books on Eihei Dogen. Their philosophical and spiritual sophistication has profoundly affected my understanding of Zen in general and the precepts in particular—and has considerably deepened my understanding of Dogen. They have also given clear and new meaning to much of my Zen experience. And special thanks, of course, to Matt Zepelin not just for his editorial skill but also for keeping me going with his firm but gentle hand. And to Sami Ripley and everyone else at Shambhala for turning these teacherly Zen and philosophical musings into a book.

List of the Zen Precepts

The Three Treasures

Buddha

Dharma

Sangha

The Three Pure Precepts

Cease from Evil

Do Good

Do Good for Others

The Ten Grave Precepts

1. Non-killing
2. Non-stealing
3. Non-misusing Sex
4. Non-lying
5. Non-misusing Intoxicants
6. Non-talking About Others' Errors and Faults
7. Non-elevating Oneself and Blaming Others
8. Non-being Stingy
9. Non-being Angry
10. Non-abusing the Three Treasures

Opening to Oneness

An Introduction to the Zen Precepts

ZEN BUDDHISM has understood its ethical teachings in a particular way, but it is a way to which anyone, regardless of tradition or lack thereof, can relate. These teachings, particularly in the Soto sect, take the form of what are called the Sixteen Bodhisattva Precepts—you can see them in the list in the front matter, where I have chosen to present them, as is often done, with *non* instead of *not* or *don't* before each one.

Bernie Glassman, my first and only Zen teacher, once said to me, "There are precepts without Buddhism but no Buddhism without precepts." Jukai, the ritual that in the US has become a rite of passage for "becoming a Zen Buddhist," is actually all about the precepts. In fact, *jukai* means "receiving the precepts." Because this precepts ceremony in the West has so often been taken to be something like acknowledgment of a "conversion" to Zen Buddhism, it clearly indicates that there is no Buddhism without precepts. As a result, it has unfortunately been assumed by some people who teach Zen but do not consider themselves Buddhist that the reverse is also true—namely, that there are no precepts without Buddhism. This being the case, the precepts have not been taught or even acknowledged in some quarters. I would like to see that change so that the true meaning of the Zen precepts becomes available not only to those who want to practice Zen without becoming Buddhists but also to everyone.

The precepts are often treated as if they were moral principles or rules of action to be followed by those engaged in Zen practice or those who consider themselves Buddhists—principles or rules that can be treated as separate from important Zen teachings such as emptiness, suchness, interpenetration, no hindrance, or the samadhi of self-fulfilling activity. This, too, I would like to see change, and I hope the practice and inquiry presented here can make at least a small contribution toward that end.

This book came about by accident. After I was empowered, as a lay teacher, to give the precepts in the Jukai ceremony and had developed a way of studying the precepts with the first group of fifteen students, one of the precept talks was transcribed and somewhere seen by a *Tricycle* magazine editor. She asked if *Tricycle* could publish it. I said yes. Then she asked if I had more. Yes. This involved having the ten talks transcribed and my reworking them somewhat for readability. Then I was presented with the idea of a book by writer, editor, friend Lorraine Kisly, who introduced me to Dave O'Neal at Shambhala Publications. Because I knew that the unusual way we did the study had been useful, I thought, Well, why not. Those ten talks, with newly added practice exercises, constitute part one of this book.

Part one functions as a kind of workbook to be used by

anyone studying the Zen precepts in preparation for the Jukai ceremony or by anyone studying the precepts just to live them. It can also be used as a workbook by anyone practicing in any tradition or even in no tradition. The talks, and the exercises suggested at the end of each talk, are not about how to be "good" and live by the precepts; rather, they challenge us to examine deeply who we are as killers, stealers, misusers of sexuality, liars, misusers of intoxicants, gossips, blamers, misers, angry people, and abusers of the Three Treasures.

As Dave explained, the *Tricycle* talks alone would not have made for a whole book, so I had to come up with an orientation to the talks that would introduce and further interpret them. I thought I had it figured out and began writing. In the meantime, I became engaged in a deep inquiry into the nature of my own experience and the meaning of *suchness* for the great thirteenth-century Japanese Zen master Eihei Dogen, who in my view is one of the four greatest philosopher-mystics who ever lived, the other three being Plotinus, Ibn'Arabi, and Meister Eckhart. Producing this book ended up taking much longer than I had expected because Dogen completely changed all kinds of things for me—my own experience, my teaching of Zen, and my way of understanding the precepts. I came to understand why the noted Dogen scholar Hee-Jin Kim calls Dogen a "mystical *realist*."[1] As we all know, Dogen is extremely difficult to understand, but thanks to certain kinds of Zen experience, my academic concentration on the later philosophy of the great twentieth-century philosopher Ludwig Wittgenstein, and Kim's splendid work on Dogen, I think I have made a few inroads. In addition, all these years later I have come to see how deeply Bernie Glassman embodied Dogen's Zen.

This book emphasizes practice, not philosophy, but the two do not have to be incompatible. Kim, for example, even while delving more and more deeply into Dogen's philosophical side, is always at pains to remind us that Dogen's philosophizing has a soteriological purpose. Interestingly, so does Wittgenstein's. *Soteriological* is a word used by academic religion scholars and theologians to refer to that aspect of a work or a tradition having to do with "salvation"—the Buddhist version, of course, being enlightenment. For Wittgenstein, who thought philosophy was like an illness that needed therapy and not more theory, it was peace. Dogen urges us to have our practice be total, whole, undivided, sincere, authentic from moment to moment. He urges us to have all of life be practice, and, surprisingly to some, that includes language, thinking, reason, and action. We are urged to make every moment, every activity, complete and lacking nothing, and we are urged never to forget that "the darkness of ignorance is inseparable from nirvana."[2] He also asks us to inquire constantly into the nature of reality, to "clarify," "study," "investigate," and "plumb its full extent." These are not intellectual exercises. Rather, they require a willingness to be open to and curious about every aspect of our experience, deluded or not. This means not thinking *about* it, whatever it is, but sinking deeper into it in a state of not knowing and total welcoming. This allows insight and genuine understanding to occur. The result is a knowing by being.

Part two of this book consists of an inquiry into the connections among a number of important Zen concepts articulated by Dogen that are not normally brought together and that shed light on what is called "the oneness of Zen and the precepts" by the Soto School of Japanese Zen. This is approached in large part by exploring the meaning of this book's title, *Opening to Oneness.*

Of the various kinds of *oneness* to be found in the spiritual traditions, it is Dogen's treatment of *suchness* and the *nonduality of duality* that is at the heart of how Zen takes the precepts. In exploring this I have mostly drawn from his masterwork *Shōbōgenzō*, often translated as *The Treasury of the True Dharma Eye*, which consists of dozens of talks and essays. Although these topics may sound daunting at the outset, all that is required of the reader is careful reading and openness. We could say, as some Zen Buddhists would, "It is (just) a finger pointing to the moon." But as Dogen would remind us, the finger *is* the moon. This is true of all Buddhist teachings, or any teachings for that matter, that come from experience.

Inquiring into this kind of experiential understanding can help us understand why the prefix *non* is used before each precept instead of the words *not* or *do not.* It will also show us why the seemingly negative way of treating the precepts in part one—by inquiring into our failures in regard to them—is crucial for understanding and living the nonduality of duality. In part two, we will also look at the surprising meaning of the Jukai ceremony and what it teaches us about how to live with the precepts.

It is hoped that after doing all the exercises with the precepts in part one and following the inquiry in part two, we will be closer to having the precepts arise naturally and spontaneously in our lives. This will be to *be one with* them, as well as, of course, to be one with those with whom we interact.

If you intend to use this book as a workbook—namely, as support for practicing with the precepts—I recommend using it with a partner or in a group. The exercises at the end of each precept talk are a spiritual method based on structured inquiry and are best done with a partner. They were inspired by what I have learned and practiced in A. H. Almaas's Diamond Approach,

Of course, one can just read the book from beginning to end without doing the exercises, or skip part two and simply read the precept talks as the readers of *Tricycle* did. Regardless of how you decide to approach the book, be sure to read the commentaries by Bodhidharma and Dogen that appear as appendices, since they are an important reference in the talks. The Bodhidharma commentaries, "One-Mind Precepts," are from an unpublished translation by my teacher's teacher, Taizan Maezumi Roshi, that circulates in the White Plum Sangha; this is the version quoted throughout the book. You can also find a version in Robert Aitken's book *The Mind of Clover: Essays in Zen Buddhist Ethics.* They are not cited there and perhaps are Aitken's own translations (included as appendix 1). The version of the Dogen commentaries, "Kyōjukaimon," used here are also thought to be a Maezumi Roshi translation, though I have made some adaptations based on John Daido Loori Roshi's translation in *Invoking Reality: Moral and Ethical Teachings of Zen.*[3]

Since *Opening to Oneness* concerns itself with only what are known as the Ten Grave Precepts, I have included, also as an appendix, an old dharma talk of Bernie Glassman's on the Three Pure Precepts.

My Approach to Teaching the Precepts

There are different ways of practicing with the precepts. The one presented here, which I and the Zen group I work with have found valuable, invites us to look deeply into the ways we fail to live up to what each precept asks of us. It has three parts: The first involves using one's imagination to extend the narrower, more literal or conventional meaning of the precept in question to cover much more than we normally think of. For example, we steal much more than money and material goods belonging to another. Needing to be the center of attention could be considered a form of stealing, as could competitiveness or thinking of enlightenment as something that could be "mine." By extending the meaning in this way, the precept in question can come alive for each of us in our individual lives in exactly the way it needs to.

Once I see the best way for me to understand the precept in question, then I can get to know myself in relation to that precept—in particular, how I fail to live up to it. This is the second part. It is a practice of no preferences, no judgments, no shoulds or shouldn'ts, no ideas of failure. It is a practice of simply allowing what is. The outcome of going deeper and deeper into seeing and compassionately allowing who I am as a killer, liar, stealer, stingy one, and so forth is that the precepts begin to manifest themselves naturally and spontaneously in my life—and this is the third part of this approach, which in truth is not so much a separate part as the natural outcome of the first two. Why this is I will explore in part two of the book. For now, we should remind ourselves that for Buddhism, the only way to free ourselves from our general shared delusions, our personal conditionings, and the sufferings we cause ourselves and others is by going through them, not by bypassing or rejecting them. As is said in the Zen tradition:

> If you fall down because of the ground,
> You must use the ground to get up.[4]

Dogen was particularly sensitive to this, and we shall rely on him in coming to understand the precepts more deeply.

Three things have influenced me in coming to this way of studying the precepts. First, I am a retired philosophy professor with a great interest in language and its complexities. Because of my past experience, particularly with the work of Wittgenstein, it comes naturally to me to be sensitive to the role of context in understanding the multiple uses of a particular word. For example, in the case of the second precept, non-stealing, we tend right away to reify it into a single meaning—say, "not taking what doesn't belong to me"—when we could be asking, "Stealing what? Money? Time? Attention? The last cookie on the plate that doesn't yet belong to anybody?" The same broadening out into multiple meanings can be done with each of the precepts. In the chapters that follow, I have tried to be as imaginative as possible in considering the many meanings each of the precepts can have, but I encourage you to discover whatever I didn't think of that might be more useful to you.

The second thing that has influenced me is that I taught for many years at a college that places great emphasis on the individual, even on the cognitive style of the individual, in order to draw out—*educate*—the deepest and best in that student. In the case of the precepts, we are all different. What I tend to steal may be different from what you tend to steal. Moreover, stealing might be the most challenging precept for me, whereas lying is for you. In addition to these kinds of differences, we are also each presented with different life situations. Anyone who has practiced Zen for a while knows that it takes some time to discover that practice is about "me." It comes from an individual place and is not some generic thing about meditating, bowing, or walking in a certain way, nor is it working with some generic thing called "ego." This is also true of working with the precepts. "But I thought Zen was about letting go of 'me,'" you might say. This is true, but we can't let go of something until we know what it is we are hanging on to. Once we know what we're hanging on to and are able to thoroughly welcome it—in fact, *be* it—it will let go of us instead of the other way around. It's important to inquire into who I am—say, in the case of stealing—in order to have the practice land where it needs to. What is it that I tend to steal? Am I an attention stealer, a time stealer, an idea stealer, or a reputation stealer? It's important to know ourselves if this practice is going to continue to deepen and to be truly about me, a requirement for the "me" to start falling away. As Dogen famously said, "To study the self is to forget the self."[5]

The third source of influence are my twenty years or so of being a student of A. H. Almaas's Diamond Approach. Two aspects of this teaching have deeply affected the Zen person in me. The first is what it means to truly acknowledge and work with our conditioning—in particular, those aspects of ourselves we'd rather not deal with. There is a real danger in the case of the precepts that we use them as a way of avoiding acknowledging the killer, the liar, the stealer, and so forth, in us in our efforts to be "good." By doing this, we miss not only an opportunity for a kind of inner transformation to take place, one that ultimately can result in the precepts manifesting naturally and spontaneously, but also knowing that whatever we suppress in ourselves we tend to oppress in others. This leads to our being judgmental of others about the very same behaviors we don't or can't acknowledge and welcome in ourselves, especially when they are not fully conscious inclinations.

The second aspect of the Diamond Approach that has made a big impression on me is the value, and perhaps necessity, of working with others in this inquiry into who we are. This involves exposure of what we hide, which turns out to be a very liberating practice. I remember years ago, when Bernie Glassman was creating all the Greyston social services for the homeless in Yonkers, he came back from a visit to a Franciscan place that worked with men suffering from drug addiction. He was very impressed with an exercise in which an individual was challenged—in fact, exposed—by the group. It sounded scary to us Zen students, so used to privacy except with the teacher. The Diamond Approach has taught me that learning to voluntarily open up with others is a very effective way to start ending the personal version of the distinction between inside and outside, not to mention self and other, and thus to experience an important aspect of oneness and true freedom. Although it is the Diamond Approach that gave me so much experience in this kind of exercise, it is in fact Bernie who started me in this way of practice. Many years ago, he and I and his wife, Sandra Jishu Holmes, developed a Zen version of the 12 Steps of AA designed to help us be more in touch with our own inner experience, sometimes negative or painful, but also to be able to share it with others.

There are several very good books about the Zen precepts and how to practice with them, so why another one? This way of working with the precepts is different from what we are used to and seems to be quite effective for all aspects of Zen practice. It doesn't replace the usual ways of studying and practicing with the precepts, which we will look at in the next section, but it might be both preliminary to and subsequent to those ways. It can also deepen and enrich the precepts' meaning and purpose in our lives, as well as enrich other aspects of our practice. The main difference is that instead of aspiring to keep the precepts, we look deeply into our failure to do so. It is this practice of allowing and, indeed, welcoming all that we tend to want to reject in ourselves and in others that opens us to oneness and the possibility of the precepts arising naturally and spontaneously.

The Three Levels of the Precepts

We have all been exposed to ethical precepts in one form or another beginning in childhood with stories like those of Pinocchio, Cinderella, Little Red Riding Hood, and even George Washington. At first, we learn the terms *good* and *bad* for various kinds of behavior. Later we add more sophisticated concepts such as *right* and *wrong*, and eventually we make a distinction between *rights* and *responsibilities*. Those of us raised in Jewish or Christian traditions or even just living in a Western country know or at least know of the Ten Commandments. Some of us may even have taken a philosophy course on ethics in college. In recent times we've also seen the development of various kinds of organizations, academic and otherwise, that concern themselves with business ethics, medical ethics, and ethics in government.

It's worth each of us asking how much we make the ethical dimension of reality part of our daily lives. I have two friends who live their lives consciously making the effort to be better human beings in the ethical sense. Every time I have lunch or dinner with either of them, I come away inspired in some way. Their kind of attention and effort is probably not typical of most of us until we take up a spiritual practice with explicit ethical teachings. In my case—in spite of having taken courses on ethics as an undergraduate and a graduate student—it was not until I encountered Zen that I started to become ethically conscious.

Precepts of any kind are typically treated as something to be followed or observed, indicating that they are somehow "out there," separate from us and needing some kind of commitment and effort on our part to be followed. It is here that the terms *should* and *shouldn't* occur. This is a dualistic and important way to treat the precepts, and it is found in Zen as well. But Zen also aims for something else.

When Bernie said to me that there is no Buddhism without precepts, he meant something much deeper than appeared in the way he put it. The Zen precepts are not thought of as having been developed by human beings as a way of managing our social and moral interactions but rather as having been revealed to Shakyamuni Buddha as intrinsic to the enlightened reality to which he awakened. Something like this can be seen in various Western answers to the big question "Where do our basic ethical norms come from?" Among the answers are God and natural law. The difference is that in Zen as well as in the mystical traditions, West and East, the answer is not just in theory or theology but is understood in terms of practice and experience. As Dogen put it, "When we sit zazen, what precept is not observed, what merit is not actualized?"[6] This is the nondual way to treat the precepts. Of course, zazen for Dogen is not just some practice we do sitting on a cushion but is enlightenment itself. We will examine this surprising position in much greater detail in part two.

Understanding that the precepts are not just ethical norms but rather expressions of enlightened reality changes our relation to them, such that when we sit in zazen, we have become one with them instead of "following" or "observing" them. Of course, it's not just precepts we are one with. It is also the other human beings—or animals or plants—we relate to with the precepts in various circumstances. Again, this is nonduality, and where the *not*—as in "do not lie, steal, kill," and so on—becomes *non*. We could say that in certain enlightened states it doesn't even occur to us to steal or lie. But what if we are not in that state? Are we just thrown back to *should* and *shouldn't*?

As time went on in my Zen practice, I personally needed to move beyond the brief and abstract way I was introduced to the precepts four decades ago. It involved what I will provisionally call three "levels." The first is a kind of absolute version—absolute in the sense of "never, ever under any circumstances" kill, lie, steal, and so forth. The Jains' wearing of mouth masks to avoid inhaling and thus killing invisible microorganisms in the air we breathe would be an example of a "never, ever" version of not killing.[7]

The second, which comes closest to our everyday understanding of morality, always accounts for context, such that, depending on the circumstances, something like killing might sometimes even be the right thing to do. The legend of Robin Hood would be an example of how context might make stealing the right thing to do. Once one brings in circumstances, however, there is lots of room for decision-making, reasons, and disagreement. This is the realm of the relative or the necessary duality of everyday life.

The third level is the realm of the absolute. Here *absolute* doesn't mean "never, ever," as in the first case, but is the realm of oneness or nonduality, and in that sense is unlike the realm of the relative. Here the precepts are no longer something separate from us, a separation normally revealed in language such as *follow*, *adhere to*, *keep*, or *observe*. Instead, they are—as indicated by Dogen's saying, "In zazen, what precept is not observed?"—intrinsic to enlightenment, to the enlightened one, as non-stealing, non-lying, and so on.

There are many examples of great sages and saints having become so identified with Ultimate Reality—or whatever it is called in their tradition—that precepts cease being separate, namely, something to be "followed," "kept," or "observed." We can see some famous examples in the following:

> Confucius: "At seventy, I could follow what my heart desired, without transgressing what was right."[8]

> Saint Augustine: "Once for all, then, a short precept is given thee: Love God, and do what thou wilt."[9]

> Christian poet-mystic Angelus Silesius: "Man, if you live in God and die to your own will, How simple it will be His precepts to fulfill."[10]

> Meister Eckhart, the great Christian philosopher-mystic: "You must penetrate and transcend all the virtues and should take virtue only in the ground, where it is one with the divine nature."[11]

Even though we weren't aware of it at the time, I suspect that all of us have had an experience of naturally and spontaneously expressing the heart of one of the precepts without the separation of a "Should I, or shouldn't I?" and without a "Why?" The question "Why?" only makes sense when there is separation between the one who acts and the precept. In those cases, there is an answer such as,

"Because it was the right thing to do." But when a precept is the expression of oneness, there is no "Why?" and no "Because . . ."

What is striking about Dogen's treatment of the precepts —indeed, his treatment of everything—is the bringing together of what I have called levels two and three, the relative and the absolute, into the nonduality of duality. This is how the precepts have come down to us through Dogen and the Soto sect, and thus are often called non-killing, non-stealing, and so forth instead of *not* killing or *don't* kill or *Thou shalt not* kill. Dogen's short commentaries, or comments actually, "Kyōjukaimon," along with Bodhidharma's comments, "One-Mind Precepts," are in this third nondual level of *non*. We might call the second level the realm of everyday morality and the adherence to ethical principles, and we might call the third the nondual spiritual level. Our temptations to steal, whether attention or a ripe peach from the farmers market, obviously involve separation from other people and from what we imagine we lack. Our efforts to overcome those temptations by commitment and effort to follow a precept also involve separation from the precept in question. Moral excellence belongs to this second level, the level of "ought," whereas a kind of nondual moral freedom in the realm of duality belongs to the third level.

From my current vantage point, all these many years later, I can see how unsatisfactory the abstractness of the quick teaching of the precepts was, in particular the abstractness of that third level. It was held up to us beginners as being from the point of view of the absolute and thus requiring the grand "enlightenment" experience. All we could do was chalk it up to mystery and have it become a gaining idea, which takes us away from engaging in Zen practices 100 percent instead of treating them as just a means to an end. In addition, there was confusion about how some well-known Zen teachers, who supposedly had had this grand experience, could afterward have engaged in behavior that, by any standard, would be called unethical. Dogen would have seen such behavior as indicating that a deeper realization was needed, one that takes us beyond the initial freedom and confidence that can result.

What is important for Zen is the realization or recognition, no matter how it comes to one, of a truth about the nature of reality and the integration of that realization into the life of the body-mind. The realization of any truth is by definition sudden, like "a sudden and unexpected sneeze," as Dogen puts it, whereas the deep integration, embodiment, or actualization of that realization is a gradual, never-ending process.[12] A typical Zen way of describing the revelation or realization is to say that it has to be "experiential" as opposed to merely intellectual. Unfortunately, the words *experience* and *experiential* can mislead students of Zen into thinking that realization is simply a matter of having a certain kind of experience. Experiences have beginnings, middles, and endings, whereas revelations or realizations of a truth are in another category altogether. The revelation, recognition, or realization of a truth has no experiential content. It's rather that the experiences "reveal" a truth. We recognize or realize it. One could say that a mystical "seeing" can trigger a "seeing that" such and such is true. It confirms for us the truths of the teachings. It is sometimes called a radical change of perspective, recognized in a momentary glimpse out of time—and hopefully brought back into our lives in time through a never-ending gradual process of actualization. Although Dogen wouldn't put it exactly this way, the great eighteenth-century Rinzai master Hakuin says the following about the actualization process:

> But even though you reach the stage of awakening [realization] without passing through steps and stages [it's sudden], if you do not cultivate practice gradually, it will be impossible to fulfill omniscience, independent knowledge, and the ultimate great enlightenment.
>
> Even though an enlightening being has the eye to see reality, without entering this gate of cultivation it is impossible to clear away obstructions caused by emotional and intellectual baggage, and therefore impossible to attain to the state of liberation and freedom.
>
> Though you see the Way clearly one day [you have realization], as long as your power of shining insight is not great and strong, you are prone to hindrance by instinctual and habitual psychological afflictions, and you are still not free and independent in both pleasant and unfavorable circumstances.[13]

The way I recommend working with the precepts is analogous to what Hakuin says about "shining insight": In the case of the precepts we need to shine the light of welcoming awareness onto the killer, the liar—the precept breaker—in us. Such illumination, called "radiant light" (*komyo*) in Zen, while uncomfortable at first, helps us see what we are hanging on to. It reveals and loosens our attachments to aspects of our conditioning so that conditioning can let go of us. So that the body-mind drops off, as Dogen puts it.

I once asked Cynthia Bourgeault, an Episcopal priest and deep wisdom teacher, why there were no "experiences"—except, of course, the Transfiguration—in the New Testament. She simply said, "The mystic 'sees,' but that is different from 'living out of.'" This response has stayed with me for a long time.

With the precepts, of course, what matters is the "living out of." But this is true of all of Zen practice or of any practice, for that matter. What Dogen saw so deeply was the dynamism of reality, appearing in the constant birth and death of each complete moment. Thus impermanence itself is Buddha-nature. This, along with what he called our "vast and giddy karmic consciousness," means that the precepts are always alive for us in both separation and oneness, in both *not* and *non*.[14] As far as Dogen was concerned, practice itself is living out of enlightenment. Doing the practices with the precepts recommended in this book opens us further and further into understanding and living what Dogen meant by the oneness of practice and enlightenment.

There are many truths to be realized and, as is clear from well-known Zen stories, many different things can trigger a sudden realization. Bernie Glassman pushed the envelope on the possibility of triggers by taking his students on street retreats to find out what it was like to be homeless, and even on a yearly retreat at Auschwitz. Walking with him at Auschwitz the second year of the retreat, he said to me, "I've seen more openings here than in a zendo." He called these trigger situations "plunges." We are plunged into situations the ordinary mind and heart cannot encompass. Working with precepts in the way recommended in this book, and doing so in the presence of others, is a plunge.

Part One
A Workbook for the Zen Precepts

Part One Introduction

Working with the Precepts by Acknowledging the Killer in Us

IT SEEMS to be a law of human nature that suppression in us of various tendencies and fears often results in the oppression of others. Racism, sexism, and homophobia are all obvious examples of this. But we don't have to go as far as that to see that anything we reject in ourselves, we then reject in others. These two rejections produce two kinds of separation. Hiding from others what I don't like about myself—or any kind of defensive self-protection, even verbal corrections of others' perceptions of us—is automatic separation. This is why it is so good to work with others. Exposing oneself as a killer, liar, stealer, and so forth is very liberating. An interesting thing happens when, instead, we engage in self-protection or self-promotion by rejecting the stealer or liar in us. We actually isolate ourselves. We close down and cut ourselves off from the whole of reality. We lose a kind of compassionate openness and lightheartedness about our own situation and therefore that of others. We feel and behave as if we have lost the vast interconnectedness in which we live our lives.

As mentioned above, Buddhism maintains that to be free of our delusions and conditioning we have to go through them and not suppress, deny, or somehow bypass them. Otherwise we will never experience true freedom and compassion. As mentioned earlier, one way this is expressed in the Zen tradition is as follows:

> If you fall down because of the ground,
> You must use the ground to get up.
> Trying to get up without the ground,
> Makes no sense.[1]

If I fall to the ground because of my lying, I have to use my lying to get up. Maybe we could think of the getting up as a form of atonement. I can't be free of lying by ignoring it or hiding it. As the word *atonement* indicates, I have to be "at one" with it. Dogen puts this the following way:

> When a demon becomes a buddha, it exerts its demoness, breaks it, and actualizes a buddha. When a buddha becomes a buddha, he/she exerts his/her buddhahood, strives for it, and actualizes a buddha. When a human being becomes a buddha, he/she exerts his/her human nature, trains it, and actualizes a buddha. You should thoroughly understand the truth that possibilities [for actualizing a buddha] lie precisely in the ways [various beings] exert their respective natures.[2]

We might say that by exerting our nature—for example, the liar in ourselves—we break it and become a buddha. I will return in part two to what it means to "break" a particular nature and become a buddha.

Bearing Witness—How to Work with a Partner or Group

The Zen Peacemaker Order, in its statement of vision and commitment to practice, names Three Tenets initially articulated by the group's founder, Bernie Glassman—Not Knowing, Bearing Witness, and Loving Action.[3] Opening to oneness with the Zen precepts requires bearing witness, which can be done only in a state of not knowing. But what does it mean to bear witness or to be in a state of not knowing? One way to understand this is in terms of being free of projection. Take the worst version of projection—bigotry. Bigotry, expressed toward an individual or group, is often defined as intolerance of others. It is actually a generalization projected onto particular people or groups. We also have our individual, familial psychological patterns and beliefs that we generalize and project onto others and ourselves. It is this that makes significant relationships sometimes very challenging. This can happen at work, with friends, or even on a bus or the road. Judgments about others and ourselves are another version. But also consider listening, and notice all the associations, judgments, opinions, and analyses that generally occur while we are listening, our minds going back and forth into the past and future. Can we just listen, just be present to the speaking of the other in a state of not knowing? Can our minds be still and open? This is what is required in working with others on the precepts. The more we practice this way, the more we are able to do it.

In a state of not knowing, we learn to bear witness not only to others but also to ourselves. This means no judgment, self-protection, or self-promotion. It means learning to allow, even to welcome, whatever arises in us. As I have heard Hameed Ali (A. H. Almaas) say, "Don't mess with your experience." When our minds are still and open to our experience instead of interfering with it by adding analyses, judgments, excuses, and so forth, we can discover things about ourselves. But more importantly, such stillness and openness allow our experience to unfold and to reveal itself to be something other than what we thought it was.

A good way of working one-on-one is with two repeating questions or prompts, something I learned in the Diamond Approach work. To use again the example of stealing, we might do the exercise in the following way: One person offers the prompt "Tell me something you steal" over and over for ten minutes, just bearing witness to the answers, perhaps saying "Thank you" after each answer. No thinking, analyzing, or cross talk. Then sides are switched and the same is done again. The same thing is done with the second question or prompt.

For each of the ten exercises following the ten chapters in this part of the book, I will suggest one of two versions of this question exercise. The first version might be to answer repeatedly the prompt "Tell me something you steal." Money, attention, reputation, or whatever comes to mind. The second question or prompt, after sides have been switched and both partners have answered the first question, might be "How do you steal?" Openly, assertively, guiltily, privately, or in any number of other ways. The answers are totally personal. They may come rapidly or very slowly—it doesn't matter. When we are present and open to whatever comes up, this kind of exercise can derail us and show us possibilities we hadn't thought of before. The second version would be to ask both questions together. An example might be "Tell me something you steal" alternating with "What lack are you remedying?" before switching sides. Both one and two together would be done for fifteen minutes each. In the instructions at the end of each precept essay, I will say either "Ask both questions separately for 10 minutes each" or "Ask questions together alternately for 15 minutes."

For each precept I also suggest a second kind of exercise—a monologue done in the presence of one, two, or more people. Here each person talks for fifteen minutes, exploring her relation to, in this case, stealing. The question might be to explore the ways that she experiences dissatisfaction or lack and noticing the stealing that might take place as if it could remedy that. Again, surprising insights can occur. The listeners just listen with no analysis, comparison, or judgment. These exercises are deep practices for the speaker and the listener. *After* doing the exercises, conversation—namely, cross-talking discussion—can take place for as long as the participants want.

A third exercise, done first on one's own and then continued maybe a day or two later with one's partner, is another fifteen-minute monologue in which each person inquires into what stands out about the precept in question. The inquiry I have in mind is not intellectual but, again, a true and total listening to whatever is present, a complete openness, a not knowing and bearing witness to one's own experience and to the speaking of the other. In all these cases, the third tenet, loving action, can emerge as compassion—toward ourselves or others.

In my sangha, the No Traces Sangha, we have studied the precepts in this way by sticking with one precept and one partner for two or three weeks. This involves practicing on one's own each week, and once a week joining up with one's partner and also a group, which could be an entire sangha or just four people, or even just two. During the weeks between meetings, while one is on one's own, a form of inquiry can be done into whatever is the most present for one about the precept in question.

The following chapters on the precepts were originally dharma talks given one at a time during retreats the first year my sangha really practiced with the precepts. They were transcribed, edited a bit for reading, and published once every three months by *Tricycle* magazine. As a result, the repetitions were not experienced as such by the *Tricycle* readers or, for that matter, by the Zen students hearing them during retreats. I have decided to leave them more or less as they were originally published. As an academic teacher for many years and as a Zen teacher, I know well the value of repetition. It allows us to see different aspects of the same thing and, most important of all, deepens our understanding. One of my favorite Zen stories is about the disciple who hears, as he has for years, the teacher say that the Buddha "spoke with a hidden meaning, but it was not concealed to Kasyapa."[4] When the disciple heard the teacher tell this for the hundredth time, he suddenly heard the hidden meaning behind his words and became enlightened. He wept and "unconsciously burst out, 'Why haven't I heard this before?'"[5]

As noted above, Bodhidharma, the First Zen (Chinese, *Ch'an*) Patriarch, and Eihei Dogen, the fifty-first, have both left short commentaries on the oneness or "non" level of our relation to the precepts. Bodhidharma's is known as "One-Mind Precepts," and Dogen's as "The Kyōjukaimon: Instructions on the Precepts." In each precept essay I have quoted the appropriate remarks from both of these commentaries, using the unpublished translations of Maezumi Roshi, my teacher's teacher. The complete lists can be found in appendix 1. Where necessary to make the commentaries clearer, I have also quoted John Daido Loori Roshi's tweaking of the translations of Maezumi Roshi, who was his teacher as well. Our full exploration of these important commentaries will come in part two.

1

Non-killing

Zen Precept #1

MOST OF US in our daily lives are not faced with choices about killing other human beings. On the other hand, those in the military are not only trained to kill but also, once in the field, have awful choices to make. These days soldiers don't have to physically face the "enemy" to have to make such decisions. Nor do they even need to be on the same continent, as the engaging 2015 movie *Eye in the Sky*—a fictional account of the complexities of drone warfare—shows us. The use of drones in modern warfare puts the operator virtually face to face with individuals in real time but thousands and thousands of miles away. One's own life is not at stake.

Few among us are faced as part of our jobs with such terrible ambiguity around the morality of killing, and so we may wonder how the first precept, non-killing, relates to us. Yet we can all imaginatively relate to the possibility. I remember in one of my philosophy classes, in a discussion about killing, a young woman said she would not kill in any circumstance whatsoever. I dreamed up the following scenario: At rush hour at the intersection of 5th Avenue and

42nd Street in New York City, a madman with an automatic rifle climbs a lamppost and starts shooting into the crowd, killing everyone in sight. I proposed to the student that she was standing next to a policeman shot dead. Would she not grab his gun and kill the madman? To my surprise, she said, "No." This is what in Zen we might call the absolute interpretation of the precept—namely, never ever kill, regardless of the context or circumstances. On the other hand, the path forward for the military personnel in *Eye in the Sky* is suddenly called into question by changing circumstances. A little girl keeps unexpectedly showing up to run errands or play with her hoop right where they intend to bomb the suicide bombers preparing for an attack.

Discussions about what's right or wrong are important and necessary, but this isn't our task in this approach to the precepts. Rather, we want to use the precepts as means to consider the various kinds of separation that occur. I once saw a father on a bike behind his ten-year-old daughter on her bike, encouraging her to run over a pigeon. Being an animal lover, I was appalled, and I let him know it. I realize now in retrospect that making him wrong was not the way to go. As Dogen says about the first precept, "Life is non-killing." Finding some way to take advantage of his daughter's and even his own inborn respect for and love of life would have been a better way to go. Not only would my own behavior have been closer to expressing a precept naturally as opposed to a should-not principle, but by encouraging a love of life I would have brought the father and daughter closer to a natural expression of the precept. Instead, it's as if I chose to kill them, or at least their behavior. Think of all the behaviors of others we want to kill instead of seeing ourselves as capable of some version of that very same behavior.

Our job with precept practice is to learn who we are as killers in a compassionate and allowing way. What about our ordinary daily lives? How does killing show up? Continuing his teaching "Life is non-killing," Dogen says, "The seed of the Buddha grows continuously. Maintain the wisdom life of Buddha and do not kill life." Bodhidharma's "One-Mind" version is as follows: "Self-nature is inconceivably wondrous. In the everlasting Dharma, not raising the view of extinction is called 'not killing.'" According to Dogen, then, killing is the failure or the refusal to maintain life. Bodhidharma adds that even the thought of extinguishing life is to kill.

What is life? Life is everything—stones, flowers, fallen leaves, persons, teeth, mice, rotting flesh, arias, books, emotions, thoughts, tickles, pains, dirty diapers, depression, walking, laughter, even the killer in us. Nothing is excluded. Once we experience being one with some particular thing or person or emotion, or once we experience the oneness of all that makes up what we call reality, we see that everything—mental or physical, sentient or not—is alive. And we see that the whole interconnectedness is alive, as if life depended on that interconnectedness. Here we can see why this precept is often thought of in terms of separation, as if it were about the killing of oneness and thus life. So, at a very fundamental level, the level of oneness, the level of the absolute, non-killing is really non-separation.

Notice how these precepts are worded, as they come

down to us from Dogen. It's not "Do not kill" or "Not killing" but rather "Non-killing." Can I be in the state of non-killing? Killing, or even thoughts of killing; separation, or even thoughts of separation—these don't occur in that state of oneness. Thoughts of not killing also don't occur in that realm of being, which Bodhidharma implies but doesn't mention. "Look at me, I'm good, I'm not killing" or "I should not kill" separate us just as much as killing does.

What is that oneness Zen talks about? The term might seem to be Zen jargon, but what is it really? Until we have directly experienced oneness, Zen tells us that it remains just an idea. But I, for one, think that there are moments when we experience it in our ordinary lives but just don't notice it. Or, if we notice it, we don't associate it with the oneness so important in Zen. Suddenly, without conscious intention, grabbing a child or distracted adult about to walk into traffic is such a moment. Another example is truly listening to someone without any of our ideas about that person occurring while we are listening. Being *absorbed in* a book, or in anything for that matter, is another. On the other hand, sometimes we're not able to *get into* a book. Our language shows us something here. An interesting case are those who get called "heroes" for having risked their lives to save other lives. The word *hero* makes no sense to them in relation to what they did, as they were so totally one with those being saved and with their actions of saving. In situations of emergency, we see the great lengths human beings will go to in order to preserve life.

Learning to pay attention to our sense of separation can teach us a lot here. What's it like? In his poem "Faith in

Mind," Jianzhi Sengcan (Japanese, Kanchi Sosan), the Third Zen Patriarch, famously said, "The Great Way is not difficult for those who have no preferences." Preferences don't have to involve attachment and rejection, but they mostly do. What happens when all day long we have our hearts set on really good Chinese food in a new, highly touted restaurant, and we get there only to discover that it's closed? What do we feel? Disappointment? Annoyance? Do I feel my attachment to this restaurant or do I suddenly want to kill it? This might seem like a long way from literal killing, but it actually isn't. Really getting to know ourselves in these seemingly more mundane situations can teach us a lot about what Dogen calls "maintain[ing] the wisdom life of Buddha."

What is not being separate from myself? Think about the words of encouragement, "Just be yourself," or the similar phrase of praise, "She is really herself." What do these phrases mean? For one thing, they mean, don't be an idea of yourself, don't rehearse what you are going to say to someone. Just be yourself *now*, whenever that "now" is. One of my favorite Zen stories is about tenth-century Chinese Master Yunmen, yelling at his monks, "When you sit, you sit with a sit-view! When you walk, you walk with a walk-view! When you eat, you eat with a bowl-view," and then taking his staff and driving them all away. The view Master Yunmen is yelling at his monks about is self-consciousness. If I am skiing downhill and conscious of how I look at the same time, I'm likely to break a leg. What am I killing? Life! The life of 100 percent, of just sitting, just walking, just eating, just skiing, just making love, or just being myself. Whenever we are self-conscious, we've split ourselves in two and taken the life out of whatever activity we're engaged in. In our narcissistic moments, we are under the delusion that we can give that life to a view of ourselves. There are, of course, many other reasons, besides our narcissism, for splitting ourselves in two. I always think of a scene in Woody Allen's movie *Annie Hall*, when Annie Hall and Allen's character, Alvy Singer, are in bed making love, and there's a double image of Annie Hall. She's not only in bed making love but also sitting on a chair watching.

Just think how often we are tempted to or actually do kill our own experience. When we begin practicing and learn how to relax into our bodies and minds, sometimes down to deep stillness, all kinds of thoughts, emotions, and sensations can make themselves known, some for the first time. When we need to hide some of this or need not to acknowledge some of it, even to ourselves, we are killing parts of ourselves. The only way to become whole and to "maintain the wisdom life of Buddha" is to welcome all those aspects of ourselves we are consciously and unconsciously trying to smother. Our efforts at smothering can't succeed. We are killing that wisdom life by not welcoming it all. To welcome fear, anger, greed, hatred, and all possible negative emotions, sensations, and thoughts gasping for breath in us, and to do so with curiosity and compassion, is to be surprised by freedom, space, love, transformation, and life!

Speaking of preferences, think about the difference in our reaction to coming upon an abandoned very young puppy, all alone and whimpering by the side of the road, and coming upon a cockroach scurrying across the kitchen counter.

As an example of knowing well the equalizing power of "the wisdom life of Buddha," consider Muriel Rukeyser's beautiful poem, "St. Roach":

For that I never knew you, I only learned to dread you,
for that I never touched you, they told me you are filth,
they showed me by every action to despise your kind;
for that I saw my people making war on you,
I could not tell you apart, one from another,
for that in childhood I lived in places clear of you,
for that all the people I knew met you by
crushing you, stamping you to death, they poured boiling
    water on you, they flushed you down,
for that I could not tell one from another
only that you were dark, fast on your feet, and slender.
    Not like me.
For that I did not know your poems
And that I do not know any of your sayings
And that I cannot speak or read your language
And that I do not sing your songs
And that I do not teach our children
        to eat your food
        or know your poems
        or sing your songs
But that we say you are filthing our food
But that we know you not at all.

Yesterday I looked at one of you for the first time.
You were lighter than the others in color, that was
    neither good nor bad.

I was really looking for the first time.
You seemed troubled and witty.

Today I touched one of you for the first time.
You were startled, you ran, you fled away
Fast as a dancer, light, strange and lovely to the touch.
I reach, I touch, I begin to know you.[1]

As noted above, our ordinary language reveals a lot about all the varieties of killing. One interesting one is "killing time." We might say, "In order to kill time at the station, I watched something on the TV channel they had going." When we need to kill time, we reveal how much we can't just be present to the life of now, to just waiting. It occurs to me that meditation is learning all about not killing time. "The suspense is killing me" might be another version of not being able to be present. There is "I could have killed you when you said that in front of her." And then we are killed by a number of things: "It bored me to death," "We nearly froze to death," "It scared me to death," and so on.

Even more interesting are all the reversals, all the ways we say that something is killing us and mean something positive by it, such as "We died laughing!" My mother was a funny woman, a real hoot. There were certain kinds of funny things she would say that always made my father respond with "You slay me." Roberta Flack's "Killing Me Softly with His Song" is a wonderful example. To say that something was "a real killer" is often meant to praise it. This is the self of self-consciousness being killed to make room for the wisdom life of Buddha.

The most striking one of all is Master Rinzai's "If you meet the Buddha, kill him!" Nagarjuna says something similar in a short verse:

> When buddhas don't appear
> And their followers are gone,
> The wisdom of awakening
> Bursts forth by itself.[2]

Any buddha I meet is separate from me and, we might say, is already dead because of my having imagined her separate from me. That kind of buddha can only be an object and hence a conceptualization of something that can't be conceptualized. Drop it. Kill it. Forget about it. We can only *be* it. We can't know it in any conventional sense, which by definition requires separation. It is only when we know mountains, rocks, presidents, flowers, or dirty diapers from the inside, by being one with them, that the wisdom life of Buddha shines forth.

This is the precept of non-killing.

Non-killing: Partner or Group Exercises

Repeating questions: Ask (1) and (2) separately for 10 minutes each. No cross talk.

1. Tell me a way that you kill.
2. Tell me a way that you experience maintaining the wisdom life of Buddha.

Monologue: 15 minutes each. No cross talk.

What are you learning about yourself working on this precept?

Discuss together as long as you like.

2

Non-stealing

Zen Precept #2

We tend to oversimplify the phenomenon of stealing. Perhaps you are not someone who has ever robbed a bank or broken into someone's house and stolen things. And perhaps words like *defrauding, swindling, embezzling, plagiarizing, cheating,* or *looting* don't resonate with your experience. Even so, stealing has a lot to do with each of us.

Stealing is taking something that is not mine and doing so with stealth so as not to get caught. It's no surprise that *steal* and *stealth* come from the same root. Ordinarily we understand *what* is stolen to be money or valuable objects such as TVs, bicycles, cars, or jewelry. But we know that ideas are stolen as well, resulting in complicated lawsuits, and these days even identities can be stolen. Unfortunately, on the internet it's not ego identities that get stolen, and the stealing is surely not for the benefit of the victim. For that we need great Zen masters who are said to be thieves because they steal our delusions. Unlike what most of the other precepts address—such as anger, blame, or stinginess—stealing can seem remote from our everyday lives, especially when we associate it only with what is illegal or criminal. As a result, this might give us the sense that we're off the hook here. After all, most of us don't steal—or so we think. But notice all the ways stealing is embedded in our language. We call a great bargain "a real steal." We steal a kiss, a glance, someone's heart, or a base in a ball game. We steal a scene, or even the whole show. These are perfectly harmless, but we also engage in forms of stealing that are harmful, both to others and to ourselves. That is what we want to consider here.

In working with this precept, non-stealing, it would be good to look at two things: the great variety of noncriminal ways in which we steal, and how "mine" or "not mine" show up in our experience. To see the latter, it's useful to ask ourselves not just when and how we steal but also when and how we feel stolen from—for example, when we accuse another of "hogging" all the whatever it is that we think we deserve some or all of. It's also useful to think about how hard it is for very young children to learn to share and to ask ourselves how much of the resistance to sharing is still with us.

One of the marks of the enlightened person is being satisfied. When we are satisfied with what we have, there is no inclination to steal. Being satisfied with what we have—money, status, possessions, looks, health, friends—might at first glance look easy. Actually, not being satisfied with any or all of those things pretty much describes the contemporary human being. But even in medieval China there were recognizable versions of this as can be seen in the following poem:

White Hair

Don't dye it, don't pull it out
Let it grow all over your head.
No medicine can stop the whiteness.
The blackness won't last out the fall.
Lay your head on a quiet pillow.
Hear the cicadas—idly incline to watch the waters
  flow.
The reason that we can't rise to this broader view
  of life
Is because, white hair, you grieve us so.[1]

Surely this is an example of not being satisfied, but where is the stealing? Notice that the one being addressed is in some sense taking what is not his, and if dyeing hair in medieval China was like what it often is now, it was mostly done "stealthily." In addition, there is the feeling of being *stolen from* when we lose the hair color we were born with. Can we be satisfied with each change in our minds and bodies as we age?

There are many other obvious examples of stealing. Think about cleaning up after yourself or even another person who'd left a mess. Crumbs on the floor, wet towels, so on and so forth. When we turn away from that, we're stealing. We're probably stealing from many things, but at the least we're stealing from the next person who comes along. When we throw trash out the window of our cars in a beautiful countryside, we're stealing from everyone. We're stealing from not only the beauty of the land but also the enjoyment of those who come after us. Or worse, when we use too much water during a drought, it's as if we're saying, "The world is mine and I can do what I want with it." Not turning off lights, we are, of course, stealing electricity. But from whom are we stealing? Everyone else. Then there is our use of fossil fuels, which involves the worst theft of all—stealing from the future of the planet and all life, including our own. Most of the time we hide it and we know it. This is stealth. And sometimes we don't know it, and we see people who appear not to know it. But still somewhere in all of us there is a moment of shame when we turn away from discarded paper on the street or a bottle or a can that we could have easily picked up.

One of the things we do in situations like that, particularly in our own living quarters, is procrastinate. We say, "Oh, well, I'll do it later," whatever it is, even though we are right there, right in front of it. How can we be said to be stealing in this case? Among other things, we are stealing time and thus are stealing from ourselves. All those procrastinations pile up. So, in one sense we are stealing from the future—from its being clean and clear of the past. But we could also think of it as stealing from the present, from being right here, right now, doing what reality is asking us to do.

I'm sure there are many ways in which we steal time, but one of them is by wasting time. We also waste other people's time. Connected with this is the stealing of attention not only from whom we want it but also from those others who are entitled to it. I might even steal satisfaction from others. I remember when I was in high school, hearing my mother use an expression I had never heard before. I had twin sisters who were six years younger and both outstanding students. On prize day, the more competitive one tended to win most of the prizes, but one year the other one took them all. Of the more competitive one I remember my mother saying that it must have "taken the wind out of her sails." That's the first time I had heard that expression, and it strikes me now that it can be taken by the one who had the wind taken out of her sails as a form of being stolen from. But notice that when we imagine ourselves being stolen from instead of doing the stealing, there is some kind of possessiveness going on, when there could be non-attachment or even generosity.

When we are jealous, envious, comparing, competing, possessive, dominating—even when we are doormats—there's some kind of stealing going on. One of the worst things that we can steal is someone else's truth. And we do this often when we can't bear to be with what's happening in another person, particularly in psychological or spiritual contexts when something is unfolding for them. We witness this phenomenon at large scale these days in the difficulty that many white people have simply being with people of color as they tell stories of experiencing racism. What's happening in the other person might be pain, anger, or fear, and when, because of some kind of discomfort on our part, we can't be there—just be there with it, bearing witness to the unfolding of that truth to that person—we thus feel some need to "fix" it. We are then, in fact, stealing something very valuable from the other. Being with someone who is dying and being able just to bear witness is such an extraordinary practice because of how much it can teach us about this precept.

Sometimes it is even something positive unfolding in another person that we find hard to tolerate. Then we might interrupt with "Oh, I've been there, too!" or we find ourselves changing the subject in some forced way.

Interrupting someone else's speaking is perhaps less serious, but even here one can be interrupting a process. As an academic teacher, I knew how important it was to help students learn how to think for themselves, to tolerate not knowing, and to bear witness to their own intellectual unfolding. The discipline for me was not to jump in out of wanting to share some happy intellectual excitement. Even that would be stealing.

We can also steal from ourselves. I can steal part of myself from the rest of me. I can be attached to part of myself. I can prefer part of myself. Actually, it is more like being attached to a self-image or what I would like to have as part of myself. In either case, when I reject parts of myself, and I am attached to the parts I like, I'm stealing from the whole. I'm stealing from wholeheartedness and the possibility of fully being. This is what happens when we use the precepts to suppress parts of ourselves—in this case, the tendency or even just the temptation to steal. Then I steal from my awareness, my welcoming, and thus my wholeness.

Dogen's commentary on this precept: "The mind and the externals are just as thus. The gate of liberation has opened." We don't add or subtract from what is, things just as they are, with grasping, rejecting, or telling stories. It just is what it is, whether it's things in the world or what is unfolding in us. When we can totally accept that, we are satisfied. This is the precept of non-stealing. I waited all morning in line for my turn, but when I got there, there were no more free tickets to Shakespeare in the Park. Can I just accept that and move on to the next thing in my day? Can I wholeheartedly accept it? Can I wholeheartedly accept the stealer, the liar, the blamer in me?

When I originally gave the talk on non-stealing that formed the basis for this chapter, I had a funny thought about the words *to rob*. I think of *robber* as a kind of childhood word for a thief. Cops and robbers. Yet adults use it, too—"We were robbed!" But there's one use of it that's particularly horrifying and that is grave robbing. Perhaps the idea of robbing a grave strikes us as violating a taboo. In some very peculiar situations, graves are even robbed of the human remains in them. But graves are robbed for other things, too. Certainly many ancient graves have been robbed of the valuables in them. This seems to us somehow the worst kind of robbery and very remote from us. But we all do something like grave robbing in regard to the past. After all, the past is dead. We rob from the grave of the past every time we can't be present. Since the past is dead, the past should be left in peace. But we rob. We steal from it every minute.

We also steal from the future. Our expectations, hopes, strivings, intentions to gain something, worrying, and so on—all of this takes us away from the present. Interesting that when we steal from the past or the future, we are actually stealing from the present—from its fullness, its hereness, its richness. Recently I thought of a good bumper sticker: "Have a past, but don't let it have you." One might say the same about the future.

We could think of sitting meditation as practice in non-stealing. It is the practice of nothing to get. That there is nothing to get is really one of the hardest things to get—and to practice. We suffer from the delusion that we lack something, and as a result, we are not satisfied. So, we end up wanting to steal from somewhere. We want to get something we imagine we don't have. We imagine that it isn't "mine" yet and we want it to be "mine." Part of the delusion is imagining that it is a question of having something we don't have, whereas the discovery is that I *am* it, not that I *have* it. In Master Keizan's *Denkoroku* there is a case about this:

> The thirty-first patriarch [China's Fourth Patriarch], the Zen master Dayi [Daoxin], bowed to the Great Master Jianzhi and said, "I beg the priest in his great compassion to give me the teaching of liberation." The Patriarch replied, "Who is binding you?" The master said, "No one is binding me." The Patriarch answered, "Then why are you seeking liberation?" With these words, the master was greatly awakened.[2]

Dayi imagines that Jianzhi has something he doesn't have, and Dayi wants it. Bodhidharma's version of this precept is apropos: "Self-nature is inconceivably wondrous. In the ungraspable Dharma, not arousing the thought of gain is called 'not stealing.'" Notice that, in the case of this precept,

Bodhidharma calls the Dharma "ungraspable." It makes no sense to want to gain or attain the ungraspable. This is why we call the belief on which that thought or desire is based a "delusion."

In addition to recognizing that the Dharma is unattainable and hence not anything we could steal, we need to notice that the delusive thought of gain always arises from a sense of lack. In this particular case, that sense of lack not only makes us want something we think we don't have but also has us wanting it *for ourselves.* That self-centered grasping for what we imagine awakening to be is a kind of delusion probably suffered by everyone at the beginning of practice. That we imagine it will be "mine" one day can be seen as a form of stealing. I remember the first time I heard someone say that we should practice for the sake of the Dharma, not for the sake of ourselves. It was unexpected, and it profoundly affected me. Of course, we also hear that practice is for the sake of others, even for saving all sentient beings. Then we have the words of the Buddha when he woke up: "Shakyamuni saw the morning star and was enlightened, and he said, 'I and the great earth and beings simultaneously achieve the Way.'" He didn't say that he alone achieved the Way.

This is the precept of non-stealing.

Non-stealing: Partner or Group Exercises

Repeating questions: Ask (1) and (2) together by alternating them for 15 minutes. No cross talk.

1. Tell me something you steal.
2. What kind of lack do you experience?

Monologue: 15 minutes each. No cross talk.

What are you learning about yourself working on this precept?

Discuss together as long as you like.

3

Non-misusing Sex

Zen Precept #3

THIS IS a time of great sexual freedom, which most people think is a good thing. Moreover, at this time in our human history, the subject of this good thing is everywhere—on the TV and internet and in newspapers, advertising, literature, movies, classrooms, jokes, and our conversations. There is no avoiding it—not that anyone wants to. Sexual misconduct is also to be found in the same places, and much more so recently thanks to the #MeToo movement. This includes both ordinary and scandalous infidelities as well as downright criminal behavior. We human beings seem fascinated by the misdeeds of others, particularly when they are sexual.

The third precept, non-misusing sexuality, probably originated in a monastic setting where celibacy was to be practiced. Among Buddhism's various traditions, the Tibetan Nyingma school and Japanese Zen are known for having married monastics and masters. There are, of course, practitioners in both these schools of Buddhism, West and East, who practice celibacy, but they are the exception and not the rule. In the Zen tradition, there are several masters who also happen to be Roman Catholic nuns or priests and hence are celibate. As Zen teachers and practitioners go, these too are the exception and not the rule, but there is much we can learn from them. The important thing about this precept is that it is about the *misuse* of sexuality. Celibacy can also be misused as an attempt to totally suppress or deny one's sexuality, and the Christian monastic orders these days are careful not to admit those who have this motivation.

If we are not in a position to misuse celibacy or tempted to engage in physically violent sexual misconduct, such as rape, or psychologically violent sexual misconduct, such as the abuse of young children, we might wonder what this precept has to do with us. In fact, it turns out to be a subtler and much more interesting precept than these examples might make us think. There are several different translations or phrasings of its subject matter, including "adultery," "impure sexuality," "sexual misconduct," "unchaste conduct," and "misuse of sex." What causes the misconduct and the impurity has been translated as "attachment," "greed," "grasping," and "desire." A consideration of some of the differences among these phrasings actually allows us to see the richness of the precept. I will look here at two ways of taking this precept: sexual misconduct and misuse of sex.

First, let's consider the notion of sexual misconduct. Misconduct invites condemnation, whether legal, moral, or social. When it comes to violence, rape is just the far end of a spectrum. Closer to the middle of that spectrum is what Robert Aitken Roshi, in his book on the precepts,

The Mind of Clover, calls "boorishness."[1] It made me laugh when I first read it because it seems like such a '50s word. Nowadays we have the word *groping*, which I think has actually become a legal term. I remember a few blind dates in college where I returned to my dorm in the dead of winter in an unheated car driven by a groper. The trip always took thirty minutes. Not pleasant! I don't know if young men are boorish anymore. Now we have date rape. In the news about a current scandal, a woman was asked if it was true that she had had a sexual encounter with so and so. She said, "Yes, it was consensual—and brutal." We may consent to a sexual encounter, but what that encounter turns out to be may not be what we expected. "Consensual" doesn't always mean mutual, shared, or mutually generous. Also, what seems consensual may not actually be so. What about sexual relations between teacher and student? Or between therapist and client? Or between two adulterers? Are these consensual? Here, perhaps what we need to look at—on both sides—is self-deception and motive, particularly unconscious motives. We then might see what the unintended consequences might be before it's too late.

When it comes to children, we don't have to look as far out on the spectrum as the crime of pedophilia. All we have to do is look around us at people we know who have been victims of familial sexual abuse, whether by an older sibling or even a parent. The statistics are quite surprising. All this is to say that there are forms of sexual violence that are much closer to home than we think. Failing to speak up in all these cases, whether we or others are the victims, is a serious breach of the third precept.

On the one hand, sexual misconduct is about our treatment of other people, in particular our conscious and unconscious taking advantage of the susceptibility of the other for our own gratification. That objectification and gratification can be emotional as well as physical, and it can range from the obvious—for example, rape—to the subtle—for example, seduction. Misuse of sexuality, on the other hand, is about my relationship to my own sexuality. If we look at the translations of the word for the causes of sexual misconduct—"greed," "attachment," "grasping," "desire"—we see some interesting differences. *Clinical sex addiction* is our contemporary term for repetitive sexual grasping, a "must have." Then there is addiction to pornography, which, thanks to the internet, is very accessible these days. One of my undergraduate students tells me that many of her male contemporaries are not only addicted to pornography but actually take most of their notions of sexual intimacy from it. She says it does not make them good lovers. In the case of desire, which sounds less harmful to the other than greed, there might be desire for someone else's spouse or partner. On the surface, acting on that desire might not appear harmful to the object of my desire, but what about the harm done to the spouse or partner of the other or to mine?

Infidelity and not speaking up about the possible abuse of others, interestingly, also belong with the next precept, non-lying. Another kind of lying is the "bad faith" in Jean-Paul Sartre's example of the woman in the movie theater who wants to hold hands with the man who is with her. Instead of acknowledging and assuming responsibility for her desire, she puts her arm on the armrest between them and treats it as an object in the hopes that he will take her hand. It is very common that we arrange for ourselves to be seduced and thus abjure the responsibility of conscious desire. Instead of lying to our partner, as in the case of adultery, we lie to ourselves.

One of the best treatments of sexuality that I know of is in a chapter titled "The Body and the Earth" in Wendell Berry's splendid book *The Unsettling of America*. On the subject of fidelity, he points out that we are all in some sense attracted to everyone. To deny that and to deny it of our partner is not fidelity but rather possessiveness. We then end up in what he calls "a sexual cul-de-sac." Most importantly, he talks about sexuality as an energy, like a renewable energy, to be used with great care and consciousness, and suggests that the so-called sexual revolution of the 1960s that made birth control so easily available has enabled us to use its various forms as a way of avoiding consciousness of our sexuality and the valuable energy it is.[2]

We might even say that sex is a sacred energy. It keeps the life of the world renewing itself everywhere. Without it we wouldn't be here. All religious traditions know this deeply, and some actually use sexual symbols and sexual practices with this sacred energy. These practices, when done with integrity, have hardly anything to do with our ordinary experience of sexuality. In fact, that sacred energy and its transformations are well known by those who engage at a deep and mature level in the practice of celibacy. It is important to realize that our human sexuality is not like animal sexuality. It is highly cognitive with many conceptual dimensions. The early-twentieth-century psychoanalyst Sigmund Freud shocked everyone by talking about the sexuality of children. Of course, what he had in mind was that force, that erotic, passionate, loving, alive, moving, energetic force. He wrote at great length about the oedipal stage of development where the child has a passionate attachment to the parent of the opposite sex and has to work out a very complicated thing in his or her development. As far as I know, no one gets through that perfectly, which contributes to the unconscious patterns found in our conditioning. Freud also reminds us that there are never just two people in bed but rather an entire family lined up on one side and another family lined up on the other side. And we can remind him that there is more gender complexity in human nature than in his neat binary picture. But whatever one's sexual or gender identity, there are still conditionings to be dealt with to liberate us into the nonmisuse of sexuality.

What would it be like to be fully in touch with, fully honoring that sacred energy of sexuality? Perhaps it is easier to ask what it is like not to be in touch with it. One thing to consider is our relationship to pleasure. We're pretty good at dealing with pain. We know that if we avoid it and want it over with, we only make it worse. Our various practices have taught us that if we can be right here, present to the pain, we will discover something about it. Even modern medicine has begun to use this wisdom. But we don't tend to think of pleasure in these terms. When it occurs, even when just eating a cookie, our attention is on having more or, in the case of sexual pleasure, on the outcome. The practice of trying to be present from moment to moment is to give up any goal. It is to give up any effort, ideas, control, self-images. It is to be fully in touch with that sacred energy and the generous sharing of it with another.

Going even deeper, there is no generosity or sharing in any sense that implies separation. As Bodhidharma's "One-Mind-Precepts" puts it, "Self-nature is inconceivably wondrous. In the Dharma of non-attachment, not raising the view of attachment is called 'not being greedy.'" John Daido Loori Roshi, one of Taizan Maezumi Roshi's successors, has rephrased this as, "In the Dharma where there is nothing to grasp, nothing to take hold of, 'not giving rise to attachment' is called the precept of refraining from misusing sexuality."[3] The translation makes it sound as if "not giving rise to attachment" and "refraining" are things that we do or ought to do. Actually, "where there is nothing to grasp," there is oneness and therefore no refraining and no not refraining. Grasping requires separation—I'm here, you're over there, and there is in me a "must have." Zen Master Dogen's version: "The three wheels—body, mouth, and consciousness (or body, speech, and mind)—are pure and clean. Nothing is desired; go the same way as the Buddhas." Namely, the Way of Oneness, which is not the same as the merging of self and other.

It's interesting to consider that a lot of language around sexuality has to do with fire: "in the heat of passion," "a burning desire," "she has a new flame." Then there is simply "warm" as a way of describing certain people. This is the fire of creation. It's not just *my* sacred energy I need to be in touch with but the fire of all creation from moment to moment to moment. It is continual creation. We are part of that, being created from moment to moment, being manifested. It is the love that burns the world into existence, and our sexuality brings us in touch with it, however we experience it—in action, celibacy, life, power, charisma, making love.

This is the precept of non-misusing sex.

Non-misusing Sex: Partner or Group Exercises

Repeating questions: Ask (1) and (2) separately for 10 minutes each. No cross talk.

1. Tell me a way you have misused sexuality.
2. Tell me a way you experience "the fire of creation."

Monologue: 15 minutes each. No cross talk.

What are you learning about yourself working on this precept?

Discuss together as long as you like.

4

Non-lying

Zen Precept #4

LYING IS something we learn not to do as small children, in part through the many children's stories about lying and its consequences. I remember well my mother reading the story of Pinocchio to me, not just as a story but as a kind of amusing warning. One of the most famous of *Aesop's Fables* is "The Boy Who Cried Wolf." Then, perhaps when we are a little older, we learn about George Washington and the cherry tree he cut down. The words attributed to the boy Washington, "I cannot tell a lie," were strong medicine for those of us who were his age when we first heard this story. The word *fib* seems to be used more for the lying we do as children and not for what we do as adults. *Fib* actually means a "trivial lie," and it comes from the same root as *fable*. Pinocchio was probably at the fibbing stage, whereas George Washington was clearly conscious of some kind of moral precept.

The lies of the adult world are much more various still. We have the interesting idea of a "noble lie" in Plato's *Republic*: the lie told to the members of various classes of citizens that being in one class and not another was somehow natural and not conventional, not up to us. In addition to the noble lie, we also have white lies, bald-faced lies, scams, swindles, bluffs, and many other failures to tell the truth. Fortunately, we have whistleblowers, too.

As adults practicing with the fourth precept, non-lying, it's important not to have a narrow view of lying. We are surrounded by lying. We lie personally to each other and to ourselves. Our whole society is full of lies: businesses lie, politicians lie, governments lie, teachers lie, students lie, doctors lie, patients lie. Imagine that we liars all suffered what happened to Pinocchio. The long noses would probably cause pedestrian traffic problems as well as require a redesign of our living and working spaces, not to mention our clothing.

Perhaps all lying is manipulating situations to our advantage, whether that advantage is protection of whatever I take myself to be or a promotion of whatever I want others to take me to be. Since the word *lying* can have such harsh connotations for us, perhaps a better term for working with this precept is simply *not telling the truth.* When it comes to our personal failures to tell the truth, there are many versions. We need to use our imagination to extend the narrower, more literal meaning of the precept in question to cover much more than we normally think of. We do this in order to find the right version for our own practice and to make the precept come alive for each of us. There is no one-size-fits-all here. As I have suggested with the other precepts, it is also important not to treat the precepts as moral principles—shoulds and shouldn'ts—independent of us and thus fodder for our superegos. The next step, after we uncover the various kinds of non-truth-tellers we are, is to welcome them, allow them, not suppress or reject them.

The following are some examples of the ways in which we fail to tell the truth: flattering; exaggerating; blaming; complaining; justifying oneself; cheating; making excuses; self-deceiving; being fake, false, or pretentious; not keeping a confidence; hiding; plagiarizing; being insincere, unfaithful, or inauthentic; not being transparent. I'm sure we can all come up with other examples. In many cases there is some kind of fear that prevents us from being totally honest, fear that we might lose something or someone, or that we might cause trouble and not be able to handle the effects of truth-telling.

Let's start by looking at one familiar pattern of behavior —promising the goods and not delivering. This, of course, could be a deliberate lie, but it could also be a form of self-deception if when we promise, we're doing so simply to remain in the good graces of the other. It could also be that we are habitually not realistic about what we can and cannot accomplish. Connected to these examples is the phenomenon of having an ulterior motive, which is also a failure to tell the truth, sometimes even to ourselves, and that can result in insincerity and lack of integrity and authenticity. Moreover, when we fail to deliver the goods, we are often tempted to make excuses. Sometimes I'm late getting to work and have a class full of students waiting for me. Often there is a genuine excuse—I'm caught behind a garbage truck on a narrow New York City street for twenty minutes, or someone has double-parked on me without leaving a phone number on the dashboard. But sometimes I'm *just late* and have no excuse. I can remember times when I was tempted to fabricate an excuse and on occasion actually did. Now I'm free enough to just be late.

Another version of not telling the truth is what Zen calls "idle talk," "aimless talk," or "rootless words." This doesn't have to be gossip or speaking ill of another; it can be simply *making* conversation instead of having a conversation. Often the motive is to make contact or keep contact with someone. This kind of talking is a waste—and as we will see, *no waste* has a deep meaning in Zen. In addition, in this kind of idle talk we don't consider the implications down the road of what we say. I remember reading about a saying in intelligence circles in Washington, DC, during World War II: "Loose lips sink ships." We might ask what loose lips sink in our lives.

In his book about the precepts, *The Mind of Clover*, Robert Aitkin Roshi says that no lying means "no complicity with lies." This refers to a very important failure to tell the truth—namely, the failure to speak up. With all the talk recently about sexual and other forms of misconduct among dharma teachers, it's surprising how little attention is paid to students failing to speak up. This is what my teacher has called "enabling." This, of course, happens in many other contexts—workplaces, families, schools—and is tied to all kinds of fears around dominant-subordinate structures and our relation to power and authority. It is a very good practice to inquire into our failure to speak up and the nature of the fears around it. It is also important to realize that telling the truth can be done without blame.

Failure to tell the truth to ourselves is one of the most

interesting forms of lying. Moreover, this aspect of the fourth precept has everything to do with how to work with any of the precepts. Think about the puzzling notion of self-deception. How could we deceive ourselves? Here we might say that there is a failure to *face* the truth. We look the other way out of shame or guilt or desire to be and to be seen as something we are not. Fully facing, getting to know, and actually welcoming the various kinds of liar that we are gives us a taste of not excluding anything, a taste of no inside, no outside. The more we can do this with no outcome or gaining idea in mind, the more truth-speaking and selflessness can naturally arise. Non-lying spontaneously arises when we are willing to hang out with, be conscious of, explore, and compassionately allow everything we are in regard to not telling the truth.

Working with the precepts in this way is itself a practice of non-lying. Once each of us sees the best way to understand the precept in question, then we can get to know ourselves in relation to our particular version of that precept. This is the welcoming part. It is a practice of no preferences, no judgments, no shoulds or shouldn'ts, no ideas of failure. It is a practice of simply allowing what is. The outcome of going deeper and deeper into seeing and compassionately allowing who we are as killers, liars, stealers, or stingy ones is that the precepts begin to manifest themselves naturally in our lives. We release our hold on self-preserving and self-aggrandizing and the separation they produce. What results is a relaxation, an opening up, a diminishing of judging both of ourselves and of others.

Practicing with the precepts in this way gives us some

insight into why they are considered the highest teaching in Zen. Over time, we might begin to glimpse or intuit the point of view (which is no point of view at all!) of One Mind and no separation. Non-lying is not not lying, for in the realm of the absolute or One Mind there is neither lying nor not lying. And here again we come to the two great Zen precept teachers, Bodhidharma and Dogen, whose commentaries direct our attention to the possibility of oneness, both with another human being and also with the precept in question. First, Bodhidharma's version of non-lying: "Self-nature is inconceivably wondrous. In the inexplicable Dharma, not expounding a single word is called 'not lying.'" If we start trying to describe what cannot be described, what is "inexplicable," we are, according to Bodhidharma, actually lying!

But we need to be careful here. It is, of course, true that Zen constantly warns us against this kind of lying. For example:

> Open your mouth—instantly wrong;
> Move your tongue—against the truth.[1]
>
> Saying "fire" won't burn your mouth;
> Saying "water" won't drown you.[2]
>
> Attached to words, one loses the reality,
> Stagnating in phrases, one is deluded.[3]

But at the same time we must not think that Zen is antilanguage. It is, after all, a very verbal tradition. Notice that in the last quotation the problem is being "attached to words" and "stagnating in phrases." The problem isn't words or phrases but our relation to them:

> Goso said, "If you meet a man on the path who has accomplished the Way, do not greet him with words or silence. Tell me how will you greet him?"

> You should not use words. You should not use no-words.
> Speak at once! Speak at once![4]

Master Joshu (Chinese, Zhaozhou) said he didn't like to hear the word *Buddha.* When asked how then he could teach, he said, "Buddha! Buddha!" This is to "speak at once," spontaneously, without dipping into the past, without planning or hoping for the future, without self-consciousness—namely, without a speaker. This is to be not "attached to words" and thus not to "lose the reality." Reality doesn't lie. It is we who lie about it when we are attached to words. This is the kind of speaking Bodhidharma is referring to, a conceptual, delineating, containing, self-conscious kind of speaking and not the kind of speaking that is pure expression, that is reality itself. A poem of Dogen's is about this:

> Not limited
> By language,
> It is ceaselessly expressed;
> So, too, the way of letters
> Can display but not exhaust it.[5]

This brings us to Zen Master Dogen's version of this precept: "The Dharma wheel unceasingly turns, and there is neither excess nor lack. Sweet dews permeate; gain the essence and gain the truth."

The whole universe being moistened with sweet dew means that nothing is excluded from being a manifestation or expression of the Dharma. Again, reality doesn't lie. One way this is said in Zen is "Everything preaches the Dharma"—even the nonsentient. But elsewhere Dogen tells us, as does the New Testament, that we don't always "have ears to hear": "If you are not willing to hear, the loudest voices could not reach your ears. If you are willing to hear, even the silent voices could reach your ears."[6] So it appears that even our listening can be a form of lying.

No excess or lack. Everything is perfect as it is, permeated with sweet dew. "I'm late," with or without an apology, depending on the circumstances, but definitely without excuses, explanations, or justifications. All of that is extra. Everything manifests the Dharma—even my own lying. In practicing with this precept or any of the precepts, can I listen without lying, can I hear the truth, the reality of who I am in relation to this precept or any of the precepts? Can I just allow it without all the extras of story and analysis? Can I not experience it as shameful or bad, deficient or lacking? Can I not lie to myself about the liar I sometimes am? The more I can do this, the more non-lying will naturally be expressed.

No separation between hearer, hearing, and the reality heard. No separation between speaker, speaking, and the reality spoken about.

This is the precept of non-lying.

Non-lying: Partner or Group Exercises

Repeating questions: Ask (1) and (2) together by alternating them for 15 minutes. No cross talk.

1. Tell me a way that you lie.
2. What is being protected by the lie?

Monologue: 15 minutes each. No cross talk.

What are you learning about yourself working with this precept?

Discuss together as long as you like.

5

Non-misusing Intoxicants

Zen Precept #5

TYPICALLY the first things that come to mind when we encounter this precept, non-misusing intoxicants, are drugs and alcohol—particularly alcohol, which in excess can make us drunk, inebriated, intoxicated. There are many words for it. Originally this precept was about not buying or selling intoxicants, where selling was considered even worse than ingesting. And it's no wonder, since the earliest meaning of the transitive verb *to intoxicate* in English is "to poison," which is what I'd be doing to others were I to sell or give them intoxicants. So what is intoxication really? Getting high—what exactly is that?

To start the inquiry, let's look at how this precept is treated in the several versions of the Ten Grave Precepts. Bodhidharma says of the fifth precept: "Self-nature is inconceivably wondrous. In the intrinsically pure Dharma, not arousing ignorance is called 'not being intoxicated.'" Dogen calls it non-being ignorant and gives it as "It has never been; don't be defiled. It is indeed the great clarity."

As these two commentaries indicate, intoxication has something to do with ignorance, defilement, delusion, darkness, and a clouding over of light or clarity. Yet we say that the fragrance of certain roses is "intoxicating." Is being intoxicated by the fragrance of a rose an example of delusion? If I hold the rose up to your nose, am I poisoning you? Surely not. Rumi, the thirteenth-century Persian poet, helps us out here by distinguishing among intoxicants in his poem "The Many Wines," which appears in *The Essential Rumi* and in many places online. It is worth finding.

Not only are there many kinds of intoxicants—"thousands of wines that can take over our minds," as Rumi puts it in his poem—but also different ways of being intoxicated. One occurs perhaps because some grace comes to us—maybe just the fragrance of the rose. A more intense version might be a post-Communion prayer from the Catholic Mass, which has in it the line, "O, blood of Christ, inebriate me." Quite different from these are the intoxications that are the result of some wanting or even craving and are thus, again from Rumi, "adulterated with fear or some urgency about 'what's needed.'"[1] There are also many different varieties of this second kind of intoxication, and not all of them are pleasant. For example, our return over and over again to destructive patterns may not be consciously pleasurable, but it has some kind of payoff, otherwise we wouldn't be doing it. We may be suffering but there is something we are getting from it. Maybe the safety of familiarity. Whatever it is, we are intoxicated by it.

What other kinds of intoxicants are there? We all know the substance category—drugs, alcohol, food, sugar, caffeine, nicotine. But there are other less obvious categories. Daydreaming, a form of tuning out, is a great intoxicant. So are blaming, analyzing, justifying, and storytelling. I need to tell my story; I need for you to know who I am, where I am, on and on . . . Or, forget about *you,* I tell the stories to myself. And if you really look, you'll be aware that we can actually get high on storytelling. Apologizing—great intoxicant. Obsessing—even better. Tuning out or sleeping. Being a victim. Being confused. One of the best is infatuation. There is a definite high there—and a clouded mind, for sure. And then there's pleasure. The odd thing about pleasure is that instead of fully enjoying what is here, being able to be fully present to it, we are busy looking for more. We miss the true depth of pleasure by being intoxicated with the possibility of more.

The most interesting one, especially for those with a spiritual practice of some sort, is our intoxication with how we can be "better" than we are. We get intoxicated with a future version of ourselves. Or just intoxicated with the future. Of course, we're often intoxicated with the past, too. And we can be intoxicated with suffering. It is really worth looking at your experience in terms of the high that's there. In fact, with all these examples, what's important for practice is to inquire deeply, to discover the "high"—especially the high disguised by a low.

Then there is the modern technology category—smartphones, wearables, massive multiplayer video games, and who knows what's next: Artificial intelligence? Virtual reality? The darkness and delusion that comes with intoxication here can go so far as to cause loss of life, as in texting while driving. The problem was bad enough already with simple TV. Thomas Merton, the great twentieth-century

Christian mystic, has the following to say: "Consider, for instance, the general atmosphere of pseudo-contemplation that pervades secular life today. The life of the television watcher is a kind of caricature of contemplation—passivity, uncritical absorption, receptivity, inertia—not only that but a gradual, progressive yielding to the mystic attraction until one is spellbound in a state of complete union."[2] In Buddhist terms we might call this a kind of "fake samadhi." On the other hand, meditation practice itself can become intoxicating, a kind of blissful tuning out where awakeness is missing. The fourteenth-century Zen Master Bassui tells us, "The true meaning of the precepts is that one should refrain not only from drinking alcohol but also from getting drunk on nirvana."[3]

All of this seems to be about me, and how I am always has an effect on others. But where are the others in this particular picture? We might agree that we get intoxicated by many different things, but surely we don't sell or give intoxicants to others. Oh yes, we do! We sell intoxicants all the time. We react. We blame. We manipulate. We seduce. We play it safe. We lie, steal, kill, and invite others to join us in speaking ill of a third person. Just look at something like joking around when it's used to avoid true contact. We are constantly inviting others into our barrel of heroin. We want others to be as untruthful as we are and to join us in that high. Connected with this is another very important kind of intoxication: feeding our narcissism. Our desire is to seduce or manipulate others into praise or mirroring of us, into seeing us. Being seen, especially the way I want to be seen, is a big intoxicant. Some people can intoxicate themselves and a whole roomful of people with their narcissistic charm. But we all can charm each other with humor, infatuation, or admiration into complete inebriation. *Narcissism* seems like such a strong, narrow word, but it is actually a weak, broad one. It is simply what takes the place of recognition of our actual True Nature —a colossal case of mistaken identity.

Often we choose some subtle intoxicant—pouring a glass of wine, hopping on Facebook, making a phone call—to avoid discomfort. But there are even subtler intoxicants. Several years ago, in a discussion about this precept, one of the members of our sitting group came up with a wonderful metaphor: "I was thinking about this idea of being intoxicated. And I was sort of feeling what it is like to be worried, to revert to being worried, and it was kind of like sucking on a hard candy, you know, with a certain flavor. I could get that flavor back whenever I needed it. So that's a strange kind of intoxicant, that familiarity, that touchstone."

Sometimes we want to alter our experience just ever so slightly. I'm sitting here. I'm uncomfortable. I want to have lunch. I focus on the thought, and it becomes a craving complete with imagined possibility. It becomes an alternative to just being here, to just having lunch come when lunch comes. It isn't lunch that is the intoxicant but the thoughts about it, the craving itself, that take us away from whatever discomfort is occurring.

What are some of the discomforts we move away from and try to avoid with intoxicants? Being wrong, the fear of being wrong, negative emotions, being alone, being without reference points, being unsure, being afraid, being without approval or mirroring, being bored or restless, being overwhelmed. You can add your own to the list. The odd thing is that some of us turn away from these uncomfortable states and reach for an intoxicant, while others of us, like the group member noted just above, actually experience the state itself as the intoxicant. We can be pulled like a magnet toward these states of mind. We indulge in them and get high on them, especially if they are part of an identity. They are like drugs.

As with the other precepts, the first and most important step in working on this one is to get to know ourselves with no judgment. In this case, it is to notice our intoxication habits, to bring our full attention to them, to be curious about them, to contemplate them in a state of openness, compassion, and wonder. Part of this practice is to discover those very subtle highs, some of which, as mentioned above, are disguised as lows. Each of us is different in this respect. Find what works for you and practice meticulous attention in getting to know it. Keep in mind that this is not about identifying addictions but rather becoming aware of the state of intoxication. Then you'll know what your particular intoxicants are. Once you find that state in yourself, ask what it does to your mind, to your awakeness.

And then look again at those words: *ignorance, defilement, delusion, darkness, a clouding over of light or clarity.* Reaching for an intoxicant to avoid what is here, to cover it up, to feel better is obviously deluded. But what about being high itself? The most striking thing about it, it seems to me, is the lack of clarity, of awakeness, of presence to what is here.

Think of the expression "I was carried away by . . ." Intoxication carries us away from what is here, from the truth. In Zen, the meditation practice of just sitting is called *shikantaza.* My favorite twentieth-century Japanese Zen master, Kodo Roshi, known as Homeless Kodo because he had no temple, had the following to say about *shikan:*

> To practice the Buddha-Way is not-to-look-aside. Be one with what you encounter right now. This is called Samadhi or Shikan (just doing something wholeheartedly). You don't eat in order to take a shit. You don't shit in order to make manure.[4]

Using intoxicants is to look aside.

What is the great brightness? The Dogen translation uses the word *clarity.* Other English words that appear for this in the Zen tradition are *great light, great clarity,* and *great brightness.* Clarity has something to do with delusion, whereas light is broader, and brightness is a particular aspect of light. That light, that brightness, the light of pure awareness we might say, is what shines through us when we are able to be completely present with what is, when we are awake and not intoxicating ourselves and others. It is the manifestation of the Buddha, of the Absolute, of the Great Brightness right here, right now, when our minds are not clouded, defiled, darkened with all that is afraid to allow that brightness to shine. Zen Master Dogen's exhilarating "Death Poem" should not be mistaken for an expression of intoxication. It is, instead, that great brightness.

Fifty-four years lighting up the sky.
A quivering leap smashes a billion worlds.
Hah!
Entire body looks for nothing.
Living, I plunge into the Yellow Springs.[5]

This is the precept of the non-misusing intoxicants.

Non-misusing Intoxicants: Partner or Group Exercises

Repeating questions: 10 minutes each. After the answer to (1), ask (2), then (1) again, and (2), over and over. No cross talk.

1. Tell me a way you intoxicate yourself.
2. What are you turning away from?

Monologue: 15 minutes each. No cross talk.

What are you learning about yourself working with this precept?

Discuss together as long as you like.

6

Non-talking About Others' Errors and Faults

Zen Precept #6

AS A TEENAGER, my brother had a funny little routine about gossip. He would begin with "I never say anything about anyone that isn't good," and then, leaning over as if to whisper in your ear, he would add, "and, boy, is this good!" Usually that was followed by something really juicy.

We find this play on words amusing because we recognize in ourselves the seemingly harmless temptation to speak ill of others and to listen to such speaking. Unlike, say, killing or stealing, this precept, non-talking about others' errors and faults, is about speaking—and doing so without even lying—which doesn't seem so serious. Yet the Gatha of Atonement, chanted every morning in Zen communities, reminds us that "all evil karma ever committed by me" arises through "body, *mouth*, and consciousness." Still, we want to say, how can speaking of others' faults be as harmful as stealing? After all, as children we learn to defend against name-calling with "Sticks and stones may hurt my bones, but names can never harm me." But how many of us can say truthfully "Names can never harm me"? How many of us are completely free of the effects of the various versions of name-calling when it's aimed at us? And don't forget, in addition to name-calling, talking about others' faults can take many forms—gossip, complaining, putting down, and passing on hearsay, among others. Putting ourselves in the shoes of the one whose faults are talked about or the one who is the subject of gossip and asking how it feels can help us see how serious this can be. In the end, it can damage whole communities.

As with all the precepts, we can take this one very literally: *never ever* speak of the faults of another. Or contextually: *sometimes* it's appropriate to speak of the faults of others depending on the circumstances. Or from the point of view of oneness, we start seeing that difference and hierarchy, which depend on separation, don't exist and therefore neither do faults or even "other." So, what's there to speak ill of?! It's interesting to look at a few different versions of this precept, not so much to consider these different levels or dimensions but simply to bring out some of its various aspects in our ordinary lives. The Bodhidharma version is "Self-nature is inconceivably wondrous. In the faultless Dharma, not talking about sins and mistakes is called not talking about others' 'faults and errors.'" John Daido Loori Roshi's tweaking of this translation refers to this precept as "*refraining from* speaking of others' errors and faults."[1] Dogen's version is "In the midst of the Buddha Dharma, we are the same Way, the same Dharma, the same realization, the same practice. Do not talk about others' errors and faults. Do not destroy the Way." Notice what we have here: Not *finding fault*, which suggests that we actually look for faults. Not *speaking of the faults of others*, which, as mentioned above, includes such forms of speaking as gossip, complaining, and passing on hearsay. Not *letting others* do it, which points to our willingness, even eagerness, to listen to such speaking. And not *expounding upon* those faults, which makes me think of the pleasure of shared "analysis" of the behavior of others—in other words, going on and on exercising our great "perceptiveness."

So, what are faults, anyway? That's worth thinking about. We should, of course, include related words such as *failings*, *foibles*, *defects*, *weaknesses*, and *shortcomings*. Foibles don't seem as serious a fault as defects of character, but talking about them may be just as harmful. But before we get to the talking-about part, notice the moralistic connotation of these words, an assumption that things or people should be other than what they are. Notice the *should* here. When we find fault, not only do we have a preference but we are ready to reject something, to exclude it from our world and definitely from ourselves. From the perspective of the Absolute, the One Body, Bodhidharma's "flawless Dharma," this is, of course, impossible or doesn't even make sense. Not only is the Dharma faultless or "flawless" but nothing can be excluded. There is no "outside." Within our relative world, however, there are faults and sometimes, in appropriate ways and circumstances, they need to be corrected. But often what we think of as faults may not be at all—especially when whatever it is is not harming others and is just something I reject in myself. "Thank God, I don't have *her* elbows!" might be an example.

So, why do we talk about others' errors and faults? What's in it for us? Well, probably a number of things. Sometimes there's the need for reassurance that I'm right. Or that I'm good. Or that I'm at least not like *that*, whatever "that" may be. It can also be a way of avoiding what I imagine will be a confrontation. It's an avoidance of telling the truth, of putting truth where it belongs. So, in speaking *about* as opposed to speaking *to* someone, we're failing to honor this precept. And that's often what we do. We're afraid. Also motivating us is the need to get someone over to our side about an issue. Most striking of all is the unconscious desire for intimacy with the one to whom I am speaking. But this is a delusion, since it is nothing but false intimacy. In fact, it's amazing to think that we use speaking about the faults of others in order to feel connected. Notice the contradiction, the delusion, here: We use, and even create, separation from one thing or person to overcome separation from another! We are afraid of genuine contact, so we find something or someone to complain about or gossip about. "Talking about" others' errors and faults is elsewhere translated as "expounding upon" them. This means telling stories about, analyzing, enjoying being very "perceptive" with another at someone else's expense, as if this shared enterprise brings us closer together.

One of the things that my teacher taught me—by catching me red-handed—was not to take hearsay for the truth, and certainly never to pass it on. Sometimes we're all too eager to make truth out of hearsay. So, why do we pass it on? Why do we accept it from someone else instead of saying "That's just hearsay" or at least wondering whether it's true? There are often situations in which our judgment, in the best sense of the word, is important and needed. One of the things to be really careful of is that we don't base it on hearsay. But most important for honoring this precept is to inquire into what motivates us to pass it on.

It's worth thinking back on how much some of us got off on speaking about what we imagined to be the errors and faults of the man who was president during 9/11 and the Iraq War. We spoke about his faults, as if we knew what they were. It's a long way from national policy to the actual character of somebody. One of the reasons we do this is frustration and maybe even fear around political issues. It's as if our concern is completely misplaced. So, we speak ill of someone. That's all we are able to do, so we imagine. It's important in our laughing, joking, and sometimes incredibly serious put-down of this human being, or whoever our latest demonized public figure is, that we ask ourselves why we're doing this. What could be done in its place? What is there that we actually know and what is there that we actually do not know? It often takes courage to find out the truth.

Speaking of someone else's errors and faults is, of course, sometimes appropriate and necessary, even part of one's job. Before I retired, I taught undergraduates in a small institution where there is a great deal of personal contact with students and enormous opportunity to help them grow. A job for any teacher is to give critical feedback. It's difficult in the beginning to learn how to do that. How do we give critical feedback? Our fear of not being able to do it, our ineptitude, is one of the things that can make us talk in a fault-finding way with someone else about the person in question. The rejecting, polarizing aspect of my thinking can be so subtle here. I once had the intention to speak to my teacher about something that was causing disorder in the sangha. A fellow student, who prided herself on knowing much about the Dharma or at least about how to behave with teachers, said, "Oh, you can't do that." I followed her advice, and I have regretted it ever since. When I look back on it, I see it as such an interesting failure on my part.

There are two things that might not occur to us in regard to this precept. One is that "speaking" here is not just speaking out loud, not just speaking to another. It's also speaking in the form of judging that goes on in our heads. It's amazing—some people walk around judging everything all the time, particularly when it comes to other people's faults or what we imagine to be faults. All of us do this some of the time. It involves having preferences and rejecting, wanting to exclude. This is connected to the second thing, our relationship to our own faults. Do we do our best to ignore our own faults altogether? Or are we painfully aware of them and want to get rid of them, to exclude them from the reality of what is? The ego, by definition in the business of separation, imagines it can change itself through more separation, by excluding parts of itself from reality. We then find these faults in others and do our best to disidentify from them through speaking ill of others.

So, how can we work with this precept? The main thing to work with is our relation to our own faults. Can we befriend them or compassionately allow them? Choose your own language. The main thing is not to suppress them, act them out, or split them off onto others. Disowning our faults or even just disparaging them only piles separation onto separation, which creates disorder not only in our local sangha but in the whole world. We can see that Plato understood this well when he tells us in his *Republic* that harmony in the state is a function of harmony in the soul. One of the translations of this precept says "Don't commit haphazard talk." This means practicing mindful speaking. There is mindful listening as well, as we see in Dogen's "not letting others" speak of faults. This means that part of my honoring this precept is helping others honor it. Useful here is a rule in a seminar I once participated in—not to complain to anyone who can't do something about what I'm complaining about and not to accept a complaint unless I can do something about it.

In those circumstances where it is appropriate and important to speak about someone's errors and faults—or better yet, *to* that person—how can we do it? The same way we do it for ourselves; it's no different. No preferences, no judgments, complete welcoming, accepting what is, compassionate allowing. They are then no longer faults in the sense of something that needs rejecting. Dogen suggests that in practicing kind speech we remember how we speak to children. We can learn something as adults about speaking to each other from noticing what's natural in us in the way we speak to children. Another thing we can practice is always asking ourselves about the suffering of the other. What kind of suffering is the other experiencing? When there are grave faults involved, it's often clear that there's some kind of suffering going on, but even with small faults, suffering is always there.

One practice is to take the person you reject the most, the one whose supposed faults you have the most temptation to talk about, and concentrate on that person's strengths, perfection, True Nature, and similarities to you. Always remember the famous saying of the Roman playwright Terence: "Nothing human is foreign to me." Or the familiar saying "There but for the grace of God go I." If we can really cultivate that feeling, that spirit, it helps to change the world. We can undergo a complete change of perspective and discover, even in a relative way, what it's like to include that which we are wanting to exclude, split off, or put down. When we see that the universe is One Body, that there is no such thing as exclusion or inclusion, then we begin to know and love things just as they are.

This is the precept of non-talking about others' errors and faults.

Non-Talking About Others' Errors and Faults: Partner or Group Exercises

Repeating questions: Ask (1) and (2) together by alternating them for 15 minutes. No cross talk.

1. Tell me a way you speak of others' errors and faults.
2. What makes you do it?

Monologue: 15 minutes each. No cross talk.

What are you learning about yourself working with this precept?

Discuss together as long as you like.

7

Non-elevating Oneself and Blaming Others

Zen Precept #7

WHAT EXACTLY is blaming? Everyone knows what it's like to blame the weather, the government, her parents, or the person who rear-ended their car, which is now costing a pretty penny. These are obvious examples, but blaming can also be very subtle. Whenever my mother misplaced or lost something, she would instantly call out, "Who took . . . !" to her four children and our father. I remember teasing her that I planned to put the words "WHO TOOK!" on her tombstone. Even though her statement has the syntax of a question, it was clearly an accusation. But even if she had asked it as a question, it would have been like the philosopher's favorite non-question—"When did you stop beating your wife?"—asked of someone who had never married.

The Bodhidharma version of this precept, non-elevating oneself and blaming others, is "The ten Dharma worlds are the body and mind. In the sphere of the equal Dharma, not making any distinction between oneself and others is called the precept of refraining from elevating oneself and blaming others." Dogen's version is "Non-elevating oneself and blaming others: Buddhas and teachers realized the absolute emptiness and realized the great earth. When the great body is manifested, there is neither outside nor inside in the emptiness. When the Dharma body is manifested, there is not even a single square inch of soil on the ground."

Clearly this precept is about there being ultimately no separation between you and me, "the equal Dharma," and "no outside or inside" of the whole, the One Body. Because blame and elevation of oneself make no sense from that point of view, we should describe this precept as *non*-blaming, instead of *not* blaming. But as we've seen with each of the precepts so far, before attaining that realization, we work with not blaming—but hopefully not just as a prohibition. A prohibition on blaming can just set up more blaming, usually of myself. Rather, it's good to get to know myself in a compassionate and accepting way as a blamer and as one who elevates myself. The more I can do that and the deeper I can go with it, the more this precept will begin to manifest naturally.

This precept has two parts that are deeply connected in ways we are often not aware of. It is this connection I want to look at in order to better understand how we can practice non-blaming. I learned a lot about blame from *The Self in Transformation*, a book by the philosopher Herbert Fingarette I used to read with my philosophy of religion students.[1] In it are two connected chapters—one on blame, and the other on guilt and responsibility—in which Fingarette shows us that an important part of our moral development is learning how to blame. When we see this in young children, it's rather cute. A child, tattling on a sibling for doing something bad or wrong, calls out, "Mommy, Mommy, Johnny's taking a cookie out of the cookie jar!" There is a certain hysterical tone to it. The enormous energy being expressed is due to the fact that there is in the accuser or blamer a desire to perform the very same action and a powerful prohibition against it—and neither is conscious. This happens because the blamer is not mature enough or strong enough to acknowledge her own wish, take the inner condemnation, and experience guilt, which is the next stage in our development. Instead, she shoots it out and puts it on someone else.

It isn't only children who do this. We adults often have very strong judgments about others, expressed with a kind of vehemence. Anti-Semitism, racism, sexism, homophobia, nationalism, and practically all the "isms" are examples of this. Homo*phobia* is really the only one correctly named, since it points to an unacknowledged fear in the one making the judgment. In these cases, there is always an identity being challenged, and judgment or blame of its opposite results. It isn't that I am merely afraid that I might be such and such that I reject in others but rather I *wouldn't be caught dead* being such and such! Many people are vehemently opposed to certain things that other people are more accepting of. There are, however, two very different ways to be opposed to something. To be strongly opposed, say, to abortion as a belief or as a principle by which I live, is one thing, but to get all worked up about it even to the point of killing by bombing abortion centers is something else entirely. In the latter case we see the kind of blame that could be the result of something as simple as my identity being intensely tied up with the pro-life tribe as opposed to the pro-choice tribe. On the other hand, its vehemence could be the result of something much more complex having to do with gender and control. What is not so obvious is that even being silently and ever-so-slightly judgmental about someone else's looks, clothing, behavior, or beliefs is also a form of blame. This can include parts of cities and even parts of our own bodies, as Muriel Rukeyser tells us in her poem "Despisals."

> In the human cities, never again to
> despise the backside of the city, the ghetto,
> or build it again as we build the despised
> backside of houses.   Look at your own building.
> You are the city.
>
> Among our secrecies, not to despise our Jews
> (that is, ourselves) or our darkness, our blacks,
> or in our sexuality   wherever it takes us,
> and we now know we are productive
> too productive, too reproductive
> for our present invention—never to despise
> the homosexual who goes building another
>
> with touch   with touch   (not to despise any touch)
> each like himself, like herself each.
> You are this.

In the body's ghetto
never to go despising the asshole
nor the useful shit that is our clean clue
to what we need. Never to despise
the clitoris in her least speech.

Never to despise in myself what I have been taught
to despise. Not to despise the other.
Not to despise the *it*. To make this relation.
with the it : to know that I am it.[2]

In every case of the kind of blame this precept concerns itself with, there is condemnation or rejection of something outside that on the inside I actually am or am afraid I might be. In the case of racism or sexism, for example, the blamer or rejecter most often isn't the same race or gender of the other, but there is an unacknowledged "I wouldn't be caught dead being that" fear in the inner rejection. The mechanism of blame is also unconscious. Johnny's sister isn't at all in touch with the fact that she is tempted to take a cookie, too. This kind of rapid, automatic shooting from the hip ranges across the spectrum from scapegoating, witch hunts, and taboos at one end to the "Who took my keys!" on the other. Blame is what happens when I don't assume responsibility for the fact that I might be the one who lost my own socks or misplaced my own keys. In practicing with this precept, especially with needing to temper a tendency to be judgmental, it's good to ask, "What am I afraid of being or becoming? What am I not tolerating in myself? What am I 'ghetto-izing' in myself?" It's also good to notice the speed with which these kinds of judgments happen. It's as if we have to get rid of something so fast that we can't even allow ourselves to see it.

Every time I blame you for being, doing, having, or wearing what my superego says is off limits, and I'm not even in touch with the rejection of something inner, there is a great lack of openness happening. I'm not only closed off to you but I am closing off or holding at bay something in myself, a fear or temptation I don't want to know about. This results in a lack of freedom, not to mention a lack of love and compassion.

What does elevating oneself have to do with this? Being engaged in better or worse, right or wrong, sets up a certain kind of hierarchy in which I place myself—very insecurely—on top. Just notice the linguistic connection between *elevating* myself and *putting down* another. And elevating oneself is intrinsically an act of creating a self and with that an "outside" and "inside." There is something else interesting about this act of elevation. When I shoot from the hip at someone for, let's say, being careless and breaking one of my good dishes, there's a quick blaming anger. There is a certain kind of hit I get from it. At that moment I'm innocent, pure, better than you, which is to say I am in some sense elevating myself even if it is hardly conscious and lasts for only a few seconds. That hit we get in blaming can happen whether it's mundane anger, such as a silent judgment about a color someone is wearing, or the splitting off of a whole group of people.

There is, of course, just the ordinary sense in which we might ask, "Who is to blame for letting the dog out?" It's sometimes necessary to pose a simple question about whose fault it is. It's important, in practicing this precept, to ask that kind of question and look closely at whether we're attacking anyone or elevating ourselves. Can we do it without blame even while quite exasperated?

But what about serious blame that is seriously deserved, like for those who carried out the Holocaust? This is quite an interesting example because there are two very different ways of blaming or condemning even Adolf Hitler. The yearly Zen Peacemakers' retreat at Auschwitz, started by Bernie Glassman, teaches us a great deal about these two ways of blaming. One way is self-serving and ultimately in the interest of my own purity, as if to say, "I have absolutely nothing in common with them." It is an elevation of myself and even gives me a hit. The other way, which may be challenging, even shocking, to contemplate for the first time with regard to something like the Holocaust, is the possibility of assigning blame without elevating the self. This is a kind of condemnation that includes the feeling, as mentioned above in relation to the sixth precept, "There but for the grace of God go I," or as the Roman playwright Terence famously put it, "Nothing human is foreign to me." The tone of this kind of blame is completely different. We know this in ourselves and see it in others.

We usually think of pacificism in terms of conscientious objection during wartime and nonviolent political protests, but nonviolence is important in our ordinary relationships as well, particularly in our speaking. For example, the peacemaking, non-blaming way of communicating, especially when we feel hurt, is to speak our truth, to express our feeling in the first person, often beginning our speaking with the phrase, "I feel . . ." Of course, often we opt for this phrase's grammatically incorrect substitute, "I feel that you . . . ," which is blame, plain and simple.

With this kind of practice we are also in the territory of what we call "giving feedback," which is a really good thing to practice. It is very difficult to do in a way that is non-blaming and non-elevating, which is why some people avoid it altogether. One of the things that makes us shy away from offering feedback is the conviction that if we open up and tell the truth, we won't be safe. Why? We are afraid to really tell the truth, to be the truth of what we are, because it's unsafe. And you're the one who makes it unsafe, or so I imagine. So where's the elevating here? I'm off the hook of truth-telling—and it's your fault. Giving feedback, criticism, or appropriate blame takes courage.

One of the most insidious kinds of self-elevation is being a victim. There are times when we actually are victims and blaming the perpetrator is appropriate, but to take on the identity of a victim and be stuck blaming is something else. Surprisingly, it is a subtle form of elevation—I'm not responsible, you are. This is giving up all freedom. I think the reason that remarkable stories of forgiveness take our breath away is that we instantly feel the liberation in the ending of boundaries, the ending of "inside" and "outside." Interestingly, the word *forgive* has nothing to do with condoning; it means "to give up resentment toward." The liberation is from the burden of our own resentment.

Herbert Fingarette describes that the next stage in moral development is guilt. Guilt is only possible when we have become strong enough to take our own blame instead of shooting it out at someone doing what we unconsciously want to do. In this case, the superego, the inner critic, turns inward and condemns our conscious or unconscious wish, which results in a feeling of guilt. We all know what it's like to walk around with feelings of guilt. We've had that experience, and it's usually because there's some kind of blaming going on of something in me. But notice here, too, that although there is more maturity, there is still separation, only this time in myself, from my own guilt. I feel it, it's there, but I don't like it.

Our development from childhood to adulthood and to spiritual maturity takes us out of blaming, through guilt, and into responsibility. The latter movement can only happen when I am willing to become one with my guilt. Here I refer to the deepest responsibility, in the sense of oneness. This is connected with the way the existentialists talk about responsibility—that we are responsible for our own conditioning. "Wait, wait," we say. "Aren't other people responsible for my conditioning? After all, they conditioned me." But I will never be free if I stay there, caught in blaming other people for my psychological conditioning or even for my serious physical injury. Some people have this relationship to their parents or other people in their childhood, but it's only by assuming responsibility for who we are that we can ever become free and fully compassionate. Like the existentialists, Fingarette has a surprising example: I'm also responsible for the earthquake that has destroyed my home! If I can assume responsibility in the deepest sense, then the truth of what's right here, of what's happening, makes freedom and compassion possible. This is what Zen Buddhists call "being with what is." "When the great body is manifested," as Dogen says, I know then that I *am* the earthquake!

None of these phenomena of blaming others and elevating oneself could occur in what Zen calls the realm of "the equal Dharma," where there is no "distinction between oneself and others," where "there is no outside or inside." But even if we have suddenly glimpsed or even deeply realized that realm, we still need the gradual practice of actualization.

In practicing with this precept, it's good to keep reminding ourselves, whether we have actually tasted it or not, that there is no inside or outside. The late Vietnamese monk and peace activist Thich Nhat Hanh's famous poem "Please Call Me by My True Names" says it all. Not only does it describe the realm of "no distinction between oneself and others" but at the end he asks to be reminded so he can "wake up" and have the door of his heart left open.

> Don't say that I will depart tomorrow—
> even today I am still arriving.
>
> Look deeply: every second I am arriving
> to be a bud on a Spring branch,
> to be a tiny bird, with still-fragile wings,
> learning to sing in my new nest,
> to be a caterpillar in the heart of a flower,
> to be a jewel hiding itself in a stone.

I still arrive, in order to laugh and to cry,
to fear and to hope.
The rhythm of my heart is the birth and death
of all that is alive.

I am a mayfly metamorphosing
on the surface of the river.
And I am the bird
that swoops down to swallow the mayfly.

I am a frog swimming happily
in the clear water of a pond.
And I am the grass-snake
that silently feeds itself on the frog.

I am the child in Uganda, all skin and bones,
my legs as thin as bamboo sticks.
And I am the arms merchant,
selling deadly weapons to Uganda.

I am the twelve-year-old girl,
refugee on a small boat,
who throws herself into the ocean
after being raped by a sea pirate.
And I am the pirate,
my heart not yet capable
of seeing and loving.

I am a member of the politburo,
with plenty of power in my hands.

And I am the man who has to pay
his "debt of blood" to my people
dying slowly in a forced-labor camp.

My joy is like Spring, so warm
it makes flowers bloom all over the Earth.
My pain is like a river of tears,
so vast it fills the four oceans.

Please call me by my true names,
so I can hear all my cries and my laughter at once,
so I can see that my joy and pain are one.

Please call me by my true names,
so I can wake up
and the door of my heart
could be left open,
the door of compassion.[3]

This is the precept of non-elevating oneself and blaming others.

Non-elevating Oneself and Blaming Others: Partner or Group Exercises

Repeating questions: Ask (1) and (2) separately for 10 minutes each. No cross talk.

1. Tell me something you blame, judge, or reject for not being the way you want it to be.

2. Tell me a way you elevate yourself by judging something else.

Monologue: 15 minutes each. No cross talk.

Explore this precept more deeply in relation to yourself.

Consider how you think of yourself as a victim.

Discuss together as long as you like.

8

Non-being Stingy

Zen Precept #8

STINGY—it's a funny word. Scrooge comes to mind. We usually think of *stingy* in terms of possessions and possessiveness—not sharing what we own, being tight with money. Notice that the word *tight* describes what it feels like to be stingy.

There are many ways of being stingy. For example, a friend of mine, someone I dearly love, is very stingy with the servings she gives to people whenever she is the hostess. It's noticeable to her guests—everything on their plates is very small. The thirteenth-century Persian poet Rumi describes stinginess perfectly in his poem "Dervish at the Door."[1] At the end of this poem, Rumi reminds us that the stingy one tries "to turn a profit from every human exchange." The One or Oneness, as we might say in Zen, never tries to turn a profit from anything at all. It wouldn't even make sense. We, on the other hand, are always trying to turn a profit from every human exchange. We are always trying to get something—admiration, love, recognition, praise, acknowledgment, even just staying connected. Bargaining is something stingy people do all the time: "I'll do this if you do that" or "I'll do this in order to get that." It's always a kind of tit for tat—conditional. Think of the notion of unconditional love. It's interesting that we usually think about how nice it would be to *receive* it. Think how we manipulate, bargain, and negotiate to turn a profit from every interaction. Much of this is subtle, unconscious habit. Even when we give, serve, love, or pay attention, we're trying to get something. Sometimes it's just to get back some of what we give.

In all these cases, one of the things we're stingy with is the possibility of doing something 100 percent. Imagine loving 100 percent. Imagine acknowledging someone 100 percent, with no thought of getting something in return, which would take part of it away and make it 70 percent, or even 20 percent. We're also stingy with the truth of what's really going on in us—what we really want. We hold on to the truth, hold it back, withhold it. We play our cards close to the chest, covering the heart.

We also try to turn a profit in our spiritual practice—to get something from it. We try to get better. We try to get enlightenment. We try to get seen for doing it right. What are we being stingy with here? Wholehearted surrender to the present moment. Just being with what is—think how stingy we are with that. Think how much we hold on. We also imagine that in practicing, what we will "get" will be ours—which is, of course, the greatest delusion of all.

In addition to treating surrender as a bargaining tool—"I'll surrender to the present moment and then get something back"—we imagine that surrender is something *we* can do. If it were wholehearted surrender, there wouldn't be anyone there to do the surrendering. So how do we surrender? How do we do this non-doing? We have to be taken, if you will. We can only prepare the conditions for being taken. Taken by what? By the present moment, by Ultimate Reality, by the Absolute, by God. And the way we prepare those conditions is by staying here now, by giving up all our negotiations, our bargaining, our "getting."

We are stingy with anything we hold on to—any person, any situation, anything that's going on in us that we are unwilling to open to. We are stingy when we're not fully participating in what's happening here and now. Imagine wholeheartedly being here, for whatever it is—a class, a meeting, a dinner, gardening, a fretting baby. We are stingy when we're withholding anything about the truth of where we are. We are stingy when we don't take risks. We are stingy when we're not compassionate. We are stingy with our tears, kind words, openheartedness, open-mindedness.

What else are we stingy with? What else do we hold on to? Security. Self-images. Pain. Suffering. Unwillingness to suffer. Being right. Truth. Love. Being a victim. Need for recognition. Time. Praise. Think of how we hang on to those things. We don't give them away; we don't share them. One of the important things that we're stingy with is gratitude. It's amazing how stingy we can be with "Thank you." Think of the gratitude expressed in grace before meals. The Zen version begins, "Seventy-two labors brought us this food. We should know how it comes to us." Are we wholehearted in knowing that and expressing our gratitude—or are we stingy?[2]

We can also be stingy with *receiving* gratitude or praise. I had a great lesson in this at age sixteen when my favorite teacher complimented me on an exam or paper. I remember exactly where I was standing, on the stairway. And I behaved like a stingy sixteen-year-old, embarrassed yet pleased at the compliment, wanting to hang on to it but making a mess of receiving it. The teacher grasped my forearm with her long, slender fingers and said, "Don't be so ungracious." I'll never forget it.

Many of Mary Oliver's poems are about being grateful for, and graciously receiving, the world. In "Have You Ever Tried to Enter the Long Black Branches," she suggests that we often treat the world as mere entertainment instead of a source of wonder for which we are deeply grateful. She writes,

> Do you think this world is only an entertainment
>   for you?
> Never to enter the sea and notice how the water
>   divides
> with perfect courtesy, to let you in! [3]

Consider what Dogen has to say about the eighth precept, non-being stingy: "One phrase, one verse, ten thousand forms, one hundred grasses, one Dharma, one realization, all Buddhas. All teachers. Since the beginning there has never been being stingy." He's talking about Ultimate Reality, the Absolute, the Faceless Fellow—Allah, the "One," as Rumi calls it. There is nothing stingy about the One. There can't be, because there is nothing "outside" it. Stinginess implies separation, but there is no separation here. When it comes to this world of multiplicity, "the One" is manifested over and over and over again, from moment to moment—there is nothing stingy there. It is a gift, given to us constantly—alive, pulsating. Love, trees, fingers, the sea and its dividing water when we step in—everything is a gift. Zen Master Keizan writes in the *Denkoroku*,

> The light of the Mind—moon, and colors of the
> eye-flower are splendid;
> Shining forth and blooming beyond time, who can
> appreciate them?[4]
>
> . . .
>
> Sourceless stream from a ten-thousand-foot cliff,
> Washing out stones, scattering clouds, gushing forth.
> Brushing away the snow, making the flowers fly
> wildly—
> A length of pure white silk beyond the dust.[5]

Look at the language here: "shining forth," "blooming," "gushing forth." That "length of pure white silk beyond the dust" displays no stinginess in its manifestation. Spring blossoms, sweeping, walking, Auschwitz, nuclear waste, life, death, our lives—all are gushing forth. Another verse from Zen Master Keizan uses my favorite image:

> That One whose whole life is extremely active and
> lively
> We call the One who raises the eyebrows and blinks.[6]

That One, the Faceless Fellow, who raises the eyebrows and blinks—what a wonderful image of this manifest world, this world of many-ness that we live in, that we are. That One whose life is extremely active and lively: nothing stingy here—or as Dogen says, "Since the beginning there has never been being stingy."

What about my life? What about myself? To not be stingy with my life, with myself, is to fully express myself at every moment—fully express everything that I am. I'm not talking about exercising one's talents or gifts. Exercising one's talents is not what fully expressing oneself means. When we are fully expressed from moment to moment, we are transparent. There is no one there to know whether talents are being exercised, much less *my* talents. Nor is it *my* life.

Not to be stingy with one's life, with one's self, with this precious short gift we've been given, is often associated with finding one's voice. Buddhism as well as other religious traditions use the example of the lion's roar. No holding back there! Voice, our primary example of non-stingy expression, also shows up as a metaphor for the manifestation of the One in many-ness in the notion that everything "preaches the Dharma." Dogen asks, in a little verse, "Are not even the sounds of the bustling marketplace, the preaching of the Dharma?"[7] No stinginess here. Everything preaches the Dharma—nuclear waste, skunks, flowers, grass—and does so fully and completely. What is, is not stingy. There is nothing withheld.

So here we are, stingy in this way and that, wanting not to be. How do we work with this? The first thing is to not be stingy in discovering who we are in relation to stinginess. We need to ask, "Where am I stingy? About what? With whom?" Can we take a good, neutral look at ourselves, with no preferences? Can we compassionately allow what is or who we are in the relative sense? Can we explore deeply enough to feel the withholding, the tightness, maybe even the fear? Can we feel safe enough, non-stingy enough, to express who we are, where we are, to another? Coming to terms with who I am in relation to stinginess—and doing so with no judgment—is one thing, but being non-stingy enough to place my stinginess right out on the table before others takes the practice even deeper.

What are we doing when we do this? What is happening? Master Sengcan, the author of the Zen poem that begins "The Great Way is not difficult for those who have no preferences," also says something in that poem about letting things "take their course." It's as if everything wants to liberate itself—to take its course—and we, out of our fear, out of our stinginess, prevent that from happening. Mary Oliver's poem "The Kookaburras" is precisely about this. In the poem, kookaburra birds, kingfishers native to Australia and New Guinea, want to be let out of their cage simply to fly away home. The speaker in the poem won't let them and pays a spiritual-psychological price:

> Years later I wake in the night and remember how I
> said to them,
> *no*, and walked away.[8]

By opening that cage door, by letting out whatever we imprison inside us, we are letting things take their course. We are not being stingy with stinginess or with who we are in regard to this or any of the other precepts. By letting the kookaburras fly away, we let them take their course and transform themselves. It is then that the precepts begin to manifest naturally.

This is the precept of non-being stingy.

Non-being Stingy: Partner or Group Exercises

Repeating questions: Ask (1) and (2) together by alternating them for 15 minutes. No cross talk.

1. Tell me a way you are stingy.
2. What you are afraid of losing?

Monologue: 15 minutes each. No cross talk.

Explore your relation to this precept.

Discuss together as long as you like.

9

Non-being Angry

Zen Precept #9

I READ AN interview with Elisabeth Kübler-Ross, the Swiss psychiatrist and teacher about death and dying, in which she said something like, "Anger is a natural human emotion, it lasts five seconds." Unfortunately, when the human ego gets involved, it lasts far longer than five seconds. One of the most famous examples is the wrath of Achilles, a super mega-anger, that begins Homer's *Iliad* and is a running theme throughout the epic. Achilles's honor has been offended by King Agamemnon, and his sustained rage determines the plot of the story. It's this sustained version of anger that is a problem for us human beings.

Shouldn't we avoid, control, or suppress even the natural five-second variety? Well, it depends. Aristotle tells us that those who do not get angry at things that ought to make them angry are considered to be foolish, and so are those who do not get angry in the right way, at the right time, or with the right people.[1] But before we go there, it would be good to look at the various forms our prohibition against anger takes and how they can cause us to misuse the ninth precept, non-being angry.

Working with any of the precepts is not about engaging the superego—namely, our inner critic. In a sense, of course, the Zen precepts are moral principles, but they aren't "out there," separate from me to be held up as standards with which I can beat myself up whenever I fall short—or, even worse, beat up others when they fall short. Nor are they moral straightjackets to be used simply to control my behavior or anyone else's. They are, instead, what the realized person does naturally. As Bodhidharma puts it, "Self-nature is inconceivably wondrous. In the Dharma of no self, not postulating self is called the Precept of Refraining from Anger." But until one reaches that point, if there is such a thing as reaching it once and for all, how do we work with this precept?

Because anger is so universal, frequent, and varied, it serves as a particularly useful model for a way of working with the precepts that liberates instead of confines us as we deepen our practice. First of all, it's important to use our imagination to move beyond an oversimplified, narrow picture of what anger is. Anger takes many forms and, as is the case with all the precepts, it's good to explore its subtle variations so that we can find out precisely what works for each of us as a practice. Think of all the words we have for anger: nouns like *rage, outrage, wrath, fury, resentment, annoyance, irritation, displeasure, indignation*; adjectives like *ticked off, pissed off, boiling mad, stewing, seeing red, annoyed, simmering*; or verbs like *blow up, snap at, hit the ceiling, get under someone's skin, losing it.* In addition to all the kinds of anger, there are different things we do with anger. For example, we suppress it, act it out, or disguise it as something else. Some of us get very angry even at ourselves, and some of us haven't the vaguest idea that we are ever angry.

It's easy to think that because anger is not a good thing, I should just practice not being angry. But that's somewhat abstract and general. It's important to be precise, personal, and honest in finding out exactly what is *my* anger. Here are questions you can use to explore your experiences of anger:

- What kind of anger is it? What is its flavor?
- When do I get angry? On what kinds of occasion?
- What happens?
- Do I get angry when I drop things? When other people drop things?
- Do I get angry when I'm being criticized? Being ignored? Not getting my way?
- Do I get angry at someone treating someone else badly?
- Do I get angry back if someone is angry at me?
- How about on the road when someone dangerously cuts in front of me? Or just gently cuts in front of me in a merging line when I've been waiting a long time for my turn?
- What's the angry language that pops out of me on those occasions?
- Do I get angry more at people or at things?

Things?!? How could one get angry at *things*, you may wonder. Well, try the computer. I remember times I've been so angry at having something I'd been working on just disappear that I've ended up banging my hands on the keyboard. My favorite example is the following: in my twenties, I had a boyfriend who, during a particularly difficult week, got so angry on discovering that a not insigificant amount of money had fallen out of his back pocket that he ripped the pocket right off his pants—while he was wearing them! I'll never forget it.

In working with this precept, we can get very precise. How do I get angry? Is it hot? Is it cold? Is it quickly discharged, or is it a slow burn? Is it suppressed, denied, or hidden? What pisses me off? What gets under my skin? Is it easier for me to be angry at strangers or at those close to me? Do I ever displace my anger onto the wrong person because it's safer? Do I direct anger at myself toward someone else? What old angers am I unaware of still festering in me? What resentments do I carry around day after day? How is my private anger different from my public anger? Do I have political anger, and do I sometimes channel personal anger toward politics?

Since we really differ in all these ways, the first step is to discover my particular version of anger instead of treating it in some generic way. Once I've explored the particularity of my anger, the next part of the practice is to get to know it more deeply. Like many emotions, anger has both a cause and an object. Its cause might be that my best vase got broken through carelessness, but the object of my anger is you. Getting to know my anger means turning my attention away from its cause and its object, and from all the stories swirling around both, to the anger itself. Getting to know it means being curious about it, not having any judgments about it, and compassionately allowing it.

Obviously, suppressing anger is a way of avoiding getting

to know it, but interestingly, so is acting out the anger. In the latter case, it's like a hot potato—I can't get rid of it fast enough. What makes us avoid getting to know the actual anger? In some cases, it's fear. Many years ago I asked a friend what her analysis had been about. She thought carefully and said, "Not being afraid of my anger." I asked her what she was afraid of, and after a few moments she said, "Blowing up." She did not mean the metaphor we use for a burst of anger but rather literally blowing up. It was an existential fear. A kind of separation anxiety also prevents us from getting to know our anger. It's almost as if we're afraid of blowing up the other person! Some of us are ashamed of our anger and can't face it or admit it. Others of us have such a powerful self-image of not being the angry type that we can't even imagine that there is anything to get to know.

Why is it important to know all this about my anger? Why not just be angry? Well, for one thing, just not being angry is easier said than done, especially when one's buttons get pushed. For another, there is no freedom in avoiding or suppressing it. Getting to know who I am as what each of the precepts addresses—who I am as a liar, a stealer, or one who gets angry and blames—and truly accepting it without any judgment is a very important step in working with any of the precepts. If nothing else, it provides some space around what needs to be worked with. The more we can do this, the more we give the precept a chance to manifest naturally. It is true that some of us need to practice not acting out our anger, but knowing when and how it shows up can be an enormous help in that practice. Some of us need to get in touch with our anger and not be so afraid or ashamed of it. Again, getting to know it, even welcoming it, is an enormous help, especially when we have the courage to talk about it with others and thus stop hiding it. For those with a self-image of never being angry, the important thing to notice is that that self-image "postulates a self" just as much as anger does.

Thich Nhat Hanh has a very beautiful thing to say about what I have called "getting to know" our anger:

> Treat your anger with the utmost respect and tenderness, for it is no other than yourself. Do not suppress it—simply be aware of it. Awareness is like the sun. When it shines on things, they are transformed. When you are aware that you are angry, your anger is transformed. If you destroy anger, you destroy the Buddha, for Buddha and Mara are of the same essence. Mindfully dealing with anger is like taking the hand of a little brother.[2]

The most important reason for getting to know our anger is that its source is a precious energy that becomes anger only when it is caught up in complex egoic patterns. This energy needs to be freed and transformed as opposed to distorted, removed, or destroyed. Depression, collapse, loss of aliveness, dependence, inability to be autonomous—all of these can result when we are unable to acknowledge and feel our anger.

Years ago I was at a small party of dharma friends, and one of the hosts mentioned that he and his partner had very different ways of getting angry. Everyone got interested, and before we knew it, someone proposed that we go around the room and say how each of us got angry or how we would get angry were we to really let loose. I sat there completely dreading it, but when it got to me, I found myself happily saying I would be like Dr. Strangelove riding the bomb ready to blow up the world! This was a surprise to me but incredibly freeing. Several years later, our small New York Zen group tried this as an exercise. Given the mature-in-age, rather staid nature of most of us, it was hilarious—an ex-husband being shot in a restaurant, a huge flood to drown everyone, stabbings, suffocatings, and, of course, Dr. Strangelove blowing up the world. What was fascinating was the effect on us. Cheeks became beautifully flushed, bodies were full of energy, and a wonderful vitality appeared in the room. We had released a life force. Tantric practices work directly with anger and its transformation, but this was simply letting go of our shame and denial.

So, what about Aristotle's remark that those who cannot be angry when they should, at whom they should, and how much they should are foolish? He seems to be saying that in certain circumstances, anger can be appropriate, justifiable, or even necessary. Here it would be good to return to Bodhidharma's version of this precept: "Self-nature is inconceivably wondrous. In the Dharma of no self, not contriving a reality of self is called 'not being angry.'" When there is no self, no self-territory to defend or construct, then there is no anger. But can there be an anger that does not come from a postulated self, an anger that is not defensive? Yes, of course. There's anger at a child who rushes out into the street, endangering her life. There is anger at cruelty, at carelessness that endangers others. My teacher once got angry at me when he realized that I had not roundly condemned the behavior of a fellow student who was in the business of making money by delivering drugs. These are the quick, five-second kinds of anger. When the five seconds are up, it's over. One might say there is a kind of cleanness, clarity, and purity to this kind of anger.

But there is also an anger that stays and stays—cleanly, clearly, and purely—until something that needs to be remedied is actually remedied. We know stories about heroic whistleblowers who were angry about chemicals being dumped in a river or about information concerning the side effects of drugs being withheld. We are grateful that they endured and persisted in their clean, pure anger. It was on behalf of all of us. Years ago, I noticed two telling headlines, one from the *New York Times* and one from *Time* magazine. The first was "New Terror Plan Angers Fire Department." This was after 9/11, and it had been decided that the police should be in charge of all possible terrorist disasters that might happen in New York City. The firefighters had always been trained to do this, so they were angry because the change seemed to jeopardize public safety. There were probably some individual firefighters whose identities were all tied up with the territory of self, but in general we can recognize this as the kind of public or institutional anger that is often appropriate. Notice that the anger is about concern for others. The other headline from *Time* magazine, complete with cover photo of Ann Coulter, an ultraconservative who has written several best-selling books, was "Ann Coulter: This Conservative Flamethrower

Enrages the Left and Delights the Right." This seems quite different. Somehow the word *enrages* gives it away.

Anger is a great teacher, as Bodhidharma's version of the precept tells us. More than anything else, it teaches us what the postulating self is and how fast it can happen, especially when we least expect it. This happens when we react to someone or something with lightning-speed anger, but also when some buried ancient anger we never knew was there wakes up and slowly takes us over. In either case, there is preference—*Not this! Not this!*—and the self is born over and over again. In the realm of the Absolute, there is no self, no other in the absolute sense of those words. But once we step off the one-hundred-foot pole, then we are here with one another to practice releasing the precious energy from the entrapment of self and to experience the oneness of many-ness. It is here that, to Thich Nhat Hanh's mindfulness practice, I would add a practice of *getting so close to my anger that I no longer know its name.* It's at that point that its cause, its object, the self being angry, and the anger itself all drop away and all that is left is the precious energy, freed at last.

This is the precept of non-being angry.

Non-being Angry: Partner or Group Exercises

Repeating questions: Ask (1) and (2) together by alternating them for 15 minutes. No cross talk.

1. Tell me something that makes you angry.
2. What kind of anger is it?

Monologue: 15 minutes each. No cross talk.

Explore your anger. What's it like? Where does it occur in your body?

What's your relation to it? What happens if you get so close to it, you no longer know its name?

Discuss together as long as you like.

10

Non-abusing the Three Treasures

Zen Precept #10

THE TENTH precept, non-abusing the Three Treasures, is so different from the others, and its language so strange, that at first it's hard to make out just what it's about. So before we go to what the "non-abusing" is about, let's look at the Three Treasures—Buddha, Dharma, Sangha.

The Three Treasures are the heart of Buddhist teachings, regardless of school, history, or culture. Becoming a Zen Buddhist or even just committing oneself in some way to Buddhist teachings, one takes refuge in the Three Treasures. These treasures or jewels, as they are sometimes called, can be understood in several different ways—for example, in what we might think of as a literal way: the Buddha being Shakyamuni Buddha, who lived a couple of thousand years ago; the Dharma being his teachings; and the Sangha being the community of disciples who put those teachings into practice. But they are also understood by Buddhism to be the three main aspects of Ultimate Reality: Buddha, the oneness; Dharma, the many-ness; and Sangha, the harmony or identity of the two. Each of the Three Treasures can also be understood in other ways as well. To master the depth and complexity of the Three Treasures is quite a study and one we will barely begin to undertake here. Instead, we want to look at what the tenth precept exhorts us to not do in relation to them.

The gentlest translation I've come across says "thinking ill of" instead of "abusing," so that the tenth precept becomes "non-thinking ill of the Three Treasures." It's puzzling. What in heaven's name could that be? Why would anyone think ill of the Three Treasures? I suppose one could think ill of Buddhism, the way some think ill of Christianity, Judaism, Hinduism, or Islam, but still it seems odd. Other translations or phrasings are even more striking: we are exhorted not to "abuse" the Three Treasures, not to "slander" them, or not to "revile," "disparage," "defame," or "defile" them. At first, these phrasings were totally puzzling to me, but then they actually got me a little closer to understanding what this precept is all about. They made me think of "Thou shalt not take the name of the Lord thy God in vain," the commandment in the Jewish and Christian traditions. Growing up, I always thought that meant that we shouldn't swear, as in "Goddamnit!" or "Christ, why did you do that!!" Later, it was Judaism that began to help me understand a particular and important meaning of this commandment. Quite simply, the word *God* is not a name in the name-object sense of name. In Judaism there are many rules about writing, miswriting, saying, or otherwise representing this word. Often it is written G-d. The twentieth-century philosopher Martin Buber, in his beautiful book *I and Thou*, says that this word was originally used in *addressing* God or in hymns of praise, and later it entered the it language where "men felt impelled more and more to think of and to talk about their eternal You as an it"—as an object that could be named and pointed to. He goes on to write, "Some would deny any legitimate use of the word God because it has been misused so much."[1]

Zen Master Dogen tells us something similar about the word *Buddha* in his fascicle "Gyōbutsu-iigi" (Majestic Bearing of the Enactment-Buddha):

> The "bonds of Buddha" means to understand enlightenment abstractly and hence to be bound by intellectual views and theoretical understanding.... This is likened to binding one's self without a rope. The rope, so long without a break, is like the vines that entwine a tree to its death, or like living vainly in the cave of the conceptual Buddha.[2]

We see here that in the Buddhist context, it is "intellectual views and theoretical understanding" that the tenth precept must be addressing. But like Buber, Dogen is more specific than that. It is what he calls "the *conceptual* Buddha"—or Dharma or Sangha—that is the problem. Here is a perhaps more typical Zen expression of this point:

> Even the mere mention of the word "Buddha" should make a man rinse his mouth for three days. If one is such a man, when he hears someone say, "The very mind is Buddha," he will cover his ears and run away.[3]

What exactly does Dogen mean by "the conceptual Buddha," and how can one be free of it? The long and complex answer to those two questions is the most fundamental teaching of the entire Zen tradition. The short version, as Dogen indicates, is that the "binding" is not just of the object—namely, what is being conceptualized, in this case the Buddha, Dharma, and Sangha—but also of the subject, the one doing the conceptualizing. Even uttering the name Buddha, much less giving a definition of it as "this very mind," is abusing the Three Treasures. Any time we say, see, or know *what* something is in the sense of it being a this as opposed to a that, we are conceptualizing or binding. We are binding by giving boundaries to whatever it is as well as to whatever it is not. Buber's way of saying this is that it becomes what he calls an "it"—namely, "*a thing among things*" which "*borders on other its.*"[4]

As described by Dogen, binding has the sense of imprisoning or obstructing the freedom of the subject, the one doing the binding. But we can also think of what Dogen calls "the conceptual Buddha" as having boundaries drawn around it to distinguish it from something else, which obstructs *its* freedom as well, at least in our conception of it. Does this mean we can't see, say, or know what Buddha is, much less what anything else is? Does it mean that we have to cover our ears, rinse out our mouths, and run from the room whenever *Buddha* or any other word is being uttered or heard? Master Joshu has an answer to that:

> Joshu addressed his assembly and said, "I do not like to hear the word Buddha."

A monk asked, "Then how does your reverence teach others?"

Joshu said, "Buddha! Buddha!"[5]

Joshu's answer is not a conceptual one. He's not comparing or discriminating Buddha from something else. He is not making it "a thing among things." So far, we could say that the tenth precept is about not conceptualizing or binding the Three Treasures and thus not binding ourselves in the process of binding them. But abusing the Three Treasures goes beyond that.

The important thing, especially in considering the precepts from Bodhidharma's and Dogen's oneness point of view, is that we *are* the Three Treasures. They are not just some set of truths and teachings "out there" for us to take refuge in and maybe avoid conceptualizing. In the Jukai ceremony of receiving the precepts, just before the actual precepts are given, the preceptor says to the recipient, "Next you will reveal yourself as the Three Treasures. . . . When once you reveal yourself as the Three Treasures, all virtues and merits will be in complete realization." Then the preceptor says, "*Be* one with Buddha," and the recipient responds, "*Being* one with Buddha," and then the same for Dharma and Sangha. This is repeated three times with each of them. Since we are the Three Treasures, we take refuge not *in* the Three Treasures but *as* the Three Treasures. In a sense, then, we are taking refuge in ourselves.

Until we experience with complete certainty who we truly are, our taking refuge is a kind of deep faith, but it is not a faith *in* something. Rather, it is the faith that allows us to be in a state of not knowing, which, when truly authentic, *is* the Buddha Treasure. Moreover, it is here that the precepts arise naturally. The Jukai ceremony says, "When once you reveal yourself as the Three Treasures, all virtues and merits will be in complete realization." This is like Dogen's "When we sit zazen, what precept is not observed, what merit is not actualized?" It's not that we don't need the precepts anymore but rather, at those truly authentic not knowing, no-separation moments—what we might call "the zazen moments in life"—the precepts arise naturally. When I quickly grab the person standing next to me on the curb who is about to step in front of a car she doesn't see, there is no sense of me and the other, not to mention any calculation about the right thing to do.

Yet even having experienced such moments, and even if one has aroused deep faith, it is likely that a sense of separation from the precept remains most of the time, and hence the ongoing need for practice. Bodhidharma's commentary on this precept gives us a way of practicing with it as we have done with the other precepts:

> Self-nature is inconceivably wondrous; in the Dharma of oneness, not raising a distinction between Buddhas and beings is called "not slandering the Three Treasures."

A dualistic view, or making a distinction or discriminating between sentient beings and Buddhas, to begin with, has the problem of making each a this as opposed to a that, which is to conceptualize or bind Buddha and whatever is not Buddha. There is, then, the binding of the one making the judgment. Any time we conceptualize something in our seeing, saying, hearing, or knowing, we are, as Dogen reminds us, binding ourselves without a rope. Conceptualizing ourselves in this way means that we are taking on an identity, even as simple a one as being a subject—the one who sees, says, hears, or knows an object. Once we do that, there is self and separation, which is certainly not the Three Treasures, nor is it "the inconceivably wondrous self-nature" to which Bodhidharma points.

Thanks to comparing mind, there can also be a kind of idealizing of the Three Treasures—"I'm just a sentient being, how could I be a buddha? How could I be the Three Treasures?"—which is simply another form of binding and abusing. As Dogen reminds us, even a horse's mouth, a donkey's jaw, and a broken wooden ladle are Buddha-nature. When we make something an object, a thing among things, we may not always be aware that we as subject have also become a thing among things. We become a subject *as opposed to* an object. We then become the one who is seeing, hearing, knowing, and naming. Because our attention is usually on the object, we are often not aware of ourselves as bound subjects. On the other hand, we can be quite aware of certain identities or conceptualizations of ourselves that we defend, promote, or compare. As mentioned in the essay on nonkilling, my favorite Zen story about conceptualizing and taking on an identity is Master Yunmen's letting his monks really have it for their self-conscious conceptual behaviors.

> Master Yunmen once seized his staff, banged it down on the seat, and said, "All sounds are the Buddha's voice, and all forms are the Buddha's shape. Yet when you hold your bowl and eat your food, you hold a 'bowl-view': when you walk, you hold a 'walk-view'; when you sit, you have a'sit-view.' The whole bunch of you behaves this way!" The master took his staff and drove them all away at once.[6]

A view is a concept, not the actual thing just as it is, not the Buddha's voice or shape. The bowl-view is then separate from me, and I myself become a "view," in this case the bowl-holding view or the eating-from-the-bowl view. What is walking-with-a-walk-view? It could be something as simple as being aware that I am walking as opposed to running. More likely, it is a more narcissistic self-consciousness—Look at me. How am I doing? Think about *kinhin*, the walking meditation part of Zen meditation. In the Soto sect, there is a precise way of doing it. For those of you who are used to this kind of walking meditation, think about any time you judged someone else for not doing it correctly, or, perhaps, for doing it better than anyone else. What we don't notice is that we are binding ourselves. We can sit with a sit-view—well, I'm sitting as opposed to standing, and isn't my posture great? Or, I just can't do this right. Or, I'm not a buddha. We can have all kinds of self-images, both positive and negative, which we promote or protect and try to hide and usually compare with our views of others. In keeping with how we've worked on the other precepts, what we need to do here is to get to know ourselves as holding views, as Master Yunmen puts it, whether of chairs, tables, bowls, other people, or ourselves. And this can be any view at all. Any time we do that, we are abusing the Three Treasures and thus ourselves as the mysterious and subtle self-nature. Since, as I've said in regard to the other precepts, we can't really let go of something until we know what we're hanging on to, let's see what some of that is.

One of the things we hate is being perceived in ways that don't accord with our self-images. Ask yourself, how has someone perceived you that was upsetting? Or just think how hard it probably was to start acknowledging being a liar, stealer, blamer, and so forth in all the exercises we've done with the other precepts. Here it might be useful to look back on those exercises to see what self-images you were protecting or hiding, and especially what it feels like to have a self-image or identity. Another place to find self-images is in one's reactivity. "What pushes my buttons?"—this is a good question to ask. The most important question of all to ask in those circumstances is, "Who am I taking myself to be?" We are clearly not taking ourselves to be the Three Treasures—as if "taking myself to be" the Three Treasures even makes sense.

What about success and failure? What is my reaction to my own success or failure? What self-images are operating here? When it comes to the other precepts, it's good to notice self-images or identities of success and failure. Do we have an idea of ourselves as never lying, always telling the truth? Or as so angry sometimes that we want to kill the person who set us off? Or as never angry? Here's a good place to look at judging. How do I judge myself?

Being judgmental of others is a dead giveaway of unconscious self-judging. It's good to be reminded of the seventh precept here—non-elevating oneself and blaming others.

"Who am I taking myself to be?" is an important question. It needs careful attention, inquiry, and effort. With practice, eventually one can ask simply, "Am I taking myself to be someone?"—anyone, it doesn't matter. Taking myself to be anyone or anything is to be conceptualizing or binding and thus to be abusing the Three Treasures—even if I am taking myself to be someone who religiously follows the precepts or a particular precept at a particular time.

Unlike Bodhidharma's commentary, which points to an example of abusing the Three Treasures by our taking ourselves to be something, Dogen's commentary on this precept has nothing to do with our taking ourselves to be anything. It's useful to go back to the example of grabbing someone about to step in front of an oncoming car to get a sense of Dogen's commentary.

> The *teisho* of the actual body is the harbor and the weir. This is the most important thing in the world. Its virtue finds its home in the ocean of essential nature. It is beyond explanation. We just accept it with respect and gratitude.

A teisho is a special kind of dharma talk, completely nondual. It is pure expression, with no separation between the one expressing and what is expressed. Listening to it as well is a practice of no separation between hearer and what is heard. To appreciate the importance of the word *express*, we might think here of a face and its expression. There is no face without an expression and no expression without a face. They are not one, but also not two.

Dogen often reminds us that human verbal, oral expression isn't the only kind. In fact, as it is said in Zen, "Everything preaches the Dharma." And, of course, preaching here is expressing, which means no separation. This means that the actual body—namely, the entire universe—is both expressing the Three Treasures and is an expression of the Three Treasures. It is constantly giving a teisho. We not only "hear" this preaching, we *are* it. Like the harbor and weir, a refuge for boats and fish, this teisho is our refuge. It is the Three Treasures, which we both are and in which we take refuge. "Its virtue finds its home in the ocean of essential nature." This is a mystery. There is no binding here, nothing conceptual. "It is beyond explanation." In a state of not knowing, "We just accept it with respect and gratitude." In that state the precepts arise spontaneously.

This is the precept of non-abusing the Three Treasures.

Non-abusing the Three Treasures: Partner or Group Exercises

Repeating questions: Ask (1) and (2) separately for 10 minutes each. No cross talk.

1. How do you conceptualize yourself and when do you do it?
2. Who are you taking yourself to be right now doing this exercise?

Monologue: 15 minutes each. No cross talk.

Keep exploring the ways you conceptualize yourself and when and why you do it.

Discuss together as long as you like.

Part Two

Exploring the Precepts through Dogen's Nonduality

Part Two Introduction

The Nonduality of Duality: From Not *to* Non

THE TITLE of this book is *Opening to Oneness.* How do we do that with the Zen precepts? Why would getting to know and even welcoming the killer, liar, and stealer in us help us open to oneness? And what exactly is oneness anyway? And what about opening?

In this second part of the book, we will try to answer these questions with some help from Dogen. Keep the precepts in mind as we go through this inquiry. In the end, we will be able to understand why in the Dogen-inspired lineages of Zen, the precepts are presented as *non*-stealing, *non*-lying, and so forth, instead of *not* stealing or *don't* steal, *not* lying or *don't* lie. This will also help us see why the Jukai ceremony of "receiving the precepts" is not about becoming a Buddhist but rather about becoming a buddha. I hope this inquiry will help you to bring the *not/non* distinction into your practice. I have provided exercises—once within a chapter, the rest at the ends of chapters—for those who are interested.

Before we continue, let's think about reading for a moment. The chapters that follow will, for some, require more effort than the dharma talks on the precepts in part one of this book. In any case, it will probably be a different kind of reading. If we read slowly, carefully, openly, allowing ourselves to be drawn into Dogen's world—our world—of the nonduality of duality, we might be surprised at the transformations that can happen.

11

Different Kinds of Oneness

THE WORD *oneness* is used in many different ways in spiritual contexts and, indeed, is understood in different ways even within the Zen tradition. For example, there is the oneness of body and mind, and—so important for Dogen—the oneness of practice and enlightenment. Then there is the experience of *being one with*—namely, the *nondual* experience of oneself *as* the whole boundless, birthless, empty reality that is our universe. The interconnectedness of everything that makes up this reality is also a oneness. Another is the oneness, "identity," or interpenetration of relative and absolute.

The Absolute, so emphasized by the early Zen patriarchs, was often called One Mind, or Buddha-nature. The *One* here is not one as opposed to two or three but is rather oneness in the sense of an absolute unity. There is nothing else but it. It is a realm of absolute formlessness. Again, the word *absolute* is important. It indicates that it's not a question of formlessness as opposed to form. After all, air is formless. It is a formlessness that in some sense transcends both form and its opposite, ordinary formlessness. At the same time, as the history of Buddhism constantly reminds us, the formlessness of One Mind is not a nihilistic nothingness. The ninth-century Chinese Zen Patriarch Huang Po describes it as follows:

> This mind, which is without beginning, is unborn and indestructible. It is not green nor yellow, and has neither form nor appearance. It does not belong to the categories of things which exist or do not exist, nor can it be thought of as new or old. It is neither long nor short, big nor small, for it transcends all limits, measures, names, traces and comparisons. . . . If you students of the Way do not awaken to this Mind substance, you will overlay Mind with conceptual thought. . . . The [experience of] the substance of the Absolute is inwardly like wood or stone, in that it is motionless, and outwardly like the void, in that it is without bounds or obstructions. It is neither subjective nor objective, has no specific location, is formless, and cannot vanish. . . . This pure Mind [is] the source of everything.[1]

Huang Po urges us to awaken to this formless mind, and then to discover that it is the source of the universe of forms:

> All the Buddhas and Bodhisattvas, together with all wriggling things possessed of life, share in this great nirvanic nature. This nature is Mind. Mind is the Buddha, and the Buddha is the Dharma.[2]

Huang Po's teaching here exemplifies the way that the early Zen patriarchs not only put emphasis on the formless One Mind but also gave their attention to the whole boundless universe of interconnected forms as the manifestation or expression of this One Mind, which is the meaning of "Dharma" in the excerpt above. The nondual experience of the whole boundless universe is, of course, important in the entire Zen tradition, but by the time we get to Dogen in thirteenth-century Japan, we find a shift in emphasis away from the whole universe of forms to the actual particulars making it up.

Oneness and Particulars

Enlightenment in its concrete expression.

—DOGEN

Dogen famously experienced the kind of awakening Huang Po emphasized as the "dropping off of body-mind," and he describes it in one of his fascicles as "the great awakening preceding the time before 'the germination of any sign.'" But what truly interests him is what he calls "enlightenment in its concrete expression."[3] Its concrete expression occurs in the realm of particulars in which we live our lives—the conceptual realm, the realm of "germinated signs."

There is an interesting difference between these two kinds of enlightenment experiences. We can experience nondually the manifestation of the One Mind, understood to be the *whole* boundless reality of interconnected forms. In fact, the *only* way to experience that boundless whole is nondually. The ordinary mind cannot take in its boundlessness. There is nothing but it, hence nothing outside it to compare it to. This includes the one who discovers she *is* the boundless whole. We can also experience nondually each of the actual particulars that make up the boundless reality, and this includes the particular that each of us is as subject of this experience. This is what it means to be "one with" a particular thing or person.

In contrast to the whole, the particulars that make up that universe can be experienced both dually and nondually. To experience them nondually is to experience and live the *nonduality of duality*, and this is what Dogen means by "enlightenment in its concrete expression." He even treats concrete particulars as perhaps the most important part of enlightenment.

As a natural extension of this emphasis, Dogen goes beyond the sentient in his consideration of enlightened nature. Whereas Huang Po—in a move that is already a departure from the Indian Buddhist tradition—includes "all wriggling things possessed of life" along with "Buddhas and Bodhisattvas . . . in this great nirvanic nature," Dogen goes further to assert that tiles, pebbles, a broken wooden ladle, or a fencepost are likewise so.

Even further, Dogen maintains that the particulars of the universe of forms don't *share in* or *have* Buddha-nature, as if Buddha-nature were separate from the universe of forms, but actually *are* Buddha-nature. None among the particulars that make up this world is excluded from being Buddha-nature, not even a horse's mouth, a donkey's jaw, or anxiety.

As a way of commenting on statements about One Mind, so important to the Zen tradition, Dogen quotes "a certain monk" who says, "Because the One Whole Mind is the Supreme Vehicle, it has been said that 'it directly points us to our human heart, so that we may see our True Nature and thereby become Buddha.'" Dogen surely selects this anonymous "certain monk," as opposed to a revered patriarch, because unlike the patriarchs, the monk doesn't go far enough in his understanding of what enlightenment is. Dogen thus adds critically,

> As far as it goes, this statement is not about the everyday functioning of Buddha Dharma, for it offers no vital path that takes us beyond self, and it is not descriptive of the everyday behavior of one's whole being. . . . And what is more, why would our venerable monk Shakyamuni have set up Teaching that has no place in the everyday functioning of those in our Buddhist family? . . . You need to recognize that what is called Buddha Mind is synonymous with the Buddha's Eye, as well as with a broken wooden ladle.[4]

What Dogen is telling us here is that Buddha Mind or Buddha-nature, so often associated with the boundless, empty whole of reality, also includes everyday functioning. This is the world of all the particulars we interact with in living our lives, which can, of course, include repairing broken wooden ladles and therefore being able to dish out the soup. Interestingly, Western philosophy didn't really see that human beings live in a world full of things they have to interact with until the twentieth century. In contemporary Zen, we can see the influence of Dogen's change of perspective in such sayings as that Zen is nothing but "chop wood and carry water." Of course, this was always true, once Buddhism came to China and Zen was born, but it took Dogen to articulate it in many ways and to show that some of deepest spiritual experiences can be with the particulars of everyday life.

And, of course, among the particulars of the universe are human beings, whose relations to one another give rise to the precepts. This means that in addition to the realization that I am the formless, featureless One Mind and its whole boundless manifestation, I can also be, in moments of realization, a broken wooden ladle, a precept, and you, as well as the absolutely particular person that I am. We will get to what that means, what the experience is like, and what it has to do with the precepts further on. For now, let's continue with Dogen's criticism of the unbalanced view of enlightenment. In the excerpt that follows, he drops the "certain monk" straw man and targets a major figure in the Zen traditions, criticizing the ninth-century Zen master Rinzai (Chinese, Linji Yixuan), founder of the Rinzai school:

> In the Buddha's Way, there is an expression of intention that is personal and an expression of True Nature that is also personal, and there is an expression of both of them that goes beyond the personal. Also, there is a way of expressing them that is personal, and there is a way of not expressing them that goes beyond the personal. When we have not yet studied the expressing of the intention that goes beyond the

> personal, then this will be an expressing of intention that has not yet reached fertile ground. When we have not yet studied the expressing of the intention that is personal, this too will be an expressing of intention that has not yet reached fertile ground. We study the expressing of intent that goes beyond any person, we study that which goes beyond the personal in expressing its intention, we study a personal expressing of intention, and we study that there is someone who expresses his intention.
>
> The strongest way that Rinzai phrased it was merely as "a real person who is beyond rank"; he still had not phrased it as "a real person who has a rank." He had not yet displayed any other ways of exploring this through his training or any other ways of putting it. Thus, we must say that he had not yet reached the field of the Ultimate.[5]

The precepts are "personal," lived and maintained by persons "of rank." Another way Dogen's emphasis on the concrete particulars of our lives shows up is in his very striking remark, mentioned in part one, "When we sit zazen, what precept is not observed?" Notice that Dogen says "*what* precept"—namely, what particular precept, or which one, is not observed? His commentary on the precepts is not about precepts in general but about each particular one.

One more particular is crucial for our understanding and practice with the Zen precepts. The circumstances in which the need for a particular precept arises are also particular. In this ever-changing, dynamic reality in which we live our lives, circumstances are different from moment to moment. This, of course, determines whether, for example, non-stealing or non-lying is called for. And although non-stealing is the obvious precept to be expressed in certain particular circumstances, if one finds oneself in a Robin Hood–type of particular circumstance, it could be stealing that is appropriately expressed.

But as we will see, deciding on a course of action in light of particular circumstances is not the same as being one with those circumstances. As I mentioned in the introduction to this book, when the third way of taking the precepts was taught to me, it seemed as if what was being said was that, when coming from the absolute, one doesn't really need the precepts much. As Augustine says, "Love God and do as you will." Dogen, on the other hand, is always in the world of our lives of particular precepts, particular situations, particular failures, and oneness with those particulars.

Partner or Group Exercises

Repeating questions: Ask (1) and (2) separately for 10 minutes each. No cross talk.

1. Tell me a way you ignore the particulars of your life—a thought, a person's expression, a soup ladle, a broken fingernail, anything.
2. Tell me a time a particular stood out or grabbed your attention.

Monologue: 15 minutes each. No cross talk.

Keep exploring how you live in generalities and the moments when you don't.

Discuss together as long as you like.

Being One with Particulars

So, the kind of oneness we are concerned with here in our consideration of the precepts is our oneness with any of the particulars of this universe. This was the oneness that Dogen so thoroughly explored. It is the oneness of subject and object wherein the subject is any one of us and the object could be one of many different things—a sight, a sound, an action, a set of circumstances, a pot, a pan, a person, a precept, or even a part of oneself.

We might say that here, there is a oneness between two particulars, but Zen says about that oneness, "Not one, not two." To be "not one" means that the oneness with the other, whatever that other is, is not a merging, dissolving, or disappearing each into the other. There is still a distinction to be made between the two, but the distinction is not conceptually experienced. It's not experienced as a separation. Experientially, it is more like an interpenetration of two nameless, borderless particulars, something our ordinary or everyday minds cannot quite imagine. *Intimacy* is a term often used in Zen for both this interpenetration of nameless, borderless particulars as well as for the interpenetration of any particular form with the formless absolute.

At the same time, the two are "not two" in the sense of not being two different entities, experienced as shaped, bordered, solid, separate, and more or less permanent, hence with a gap between them—one here and the other one over there. They are no longer conceptualized objects separated from each other, nor are they separated subject and object in any conventional sense.

So often in Zen contexts we hear emphasis placed on *interconnectedness*, but when it comes to oneness, it is *interpenetration* that is important. *Penetrate* is an important term for Zen, and particularly for Dogen: "Only when one encounters things penetratingly is one genuinely free in the very act of encountering."[6] He calls the Zen path "the vital path of penetration,"[7] or in another translation, "the vigorous road of penetration and liberation."[8]

What I've said so far can sound pretty abstract. In order to get a sense of what "being one with" could mean in the case of particulars and how it affects both subject and object, I used to use an example with my undergraduate students from their everyday experience—two ways of doing one's homework in the library. In the first case, I am in a little study room with the door shut, distracted, and I *can't get into* the book. Notice our language here. When I *can't get into it*, both the book and I are experienced as bordered forms that we most likely take to be solid, in some sense permanent, and definitely separate. And, of course, that includes the desk, the coffee mug, the walls, what's on the other side of the walls, and so on. There is separation here, as well as an inside and an outside of the room, and of everything else, including the one not able to get into the book. It even includes time, which in such circumstances is experienced as flowing like molasses and, interestingly, separate from me and the objects present, as if time were a background, a container, or something flowing by.

In the second case, I am, as we say, *totally absorbed in* the book. We also say, I was *completely lost in* something. Again, notice our language. I am, in this case, "one with" the book. Being absorbed in it completely changes my experience. If I reflect back on it, I realize that I was no longer separate from the book, no longer experiencing a gap between me and the book, but it wasn't as if the book and I merged or dissolved into each other such that we disappeared. Rather, we became formless forms, which to the ordinary mind seems like a contradiction. In such cases, there is no shape or border either to me or to the book, but because we don't lose our particularity, we interpenetrate instead of merge and disappear. We keep on reading a *book* even though the reader and the book are no longer separate, hence also no longer conceptually describable. This is the kind of experience Dogen calls "the total experience of a single thing"—which, he adds, "does not deprive a thing of its own unique particularity."[9]

If I think back on my experience of the room in this second case, I realize that there was no border or boundary to it either, so that there was no "other side" to its walls. I also had no sense of myself with an inside and an outside. Time itself completely changes. It is as if no time has passed at all, almost as if it wasn't there. Who am I in this experience? Definitely not any describable me-object of self-consciousness. What am I holding in my hands? Again, nothing experientially bordered and describable. The book and I are still the particulars we are, but we can't be described, because we are now experienced as absolutely particular.

Zen has several ways of talking about this. We could call it "being in the now" or functioning in the "nonconceptual" realm. What makes this—whether it is myself, an object, another person, a thought, even a precept—a nonconceptual experience is that it is not experienced as "this, not that." There is no comparing or contrasting here. As a result, it has no name or description and can't be known as we ordinarily understand knowing something. Nonetheless, in a nondual kind of knowing, different from our usual ways, I do "know" what it is. All one can say, however, were one aware of one's experience at the time it is happening, is that it is *just this.* To have another sip of coffee in this state or in this kind of knowing, I reach for the mug and don't try to take the sip from the pen or the book. In this nondual knowing—or *prajna,* as Zen calls it—I "know" which is which, even though the describable, nameable *whatness* of the items in the room is gone. In addition, the knowing is not "mine." Both the object known in the ordinary sense *and* the subject that I ordinarily take myself to be are gone. We have become formless forms, no longer solid, separate, and permanent. I am experiencing here what Zen calls the "suchness" of the mug and of myself as well—even if I am not aware of it. Suchness is not a thing or a quality of a thing but rather the way the nonconceptual presents itself to us, and it is often translated as "as it is" or as "just this."

Even though we human beings, of necessity, live largely in the conceptual realm, we do have experiences like these, even though we typically haven't awakened to them, which is to say we are not aware of them while they are occurring. My description here of a particular kind of experience of oneness is, of course, a conceptual reflecting back on a pre-reflective, nonconceptual experience. Even though this kind of reflecting back on the pre-reflective is conceptual and can't reproduce the actual experience, it can show us both that reality can present itself in ways other than the usual, dualistic ways and that we can in some sense know something in nonconceptual, nondual ways. Our awakening to it while it is occurring, however, is a matter of grace, as some would say, after lots of practice. We can't conceptually bring about experiences of being awake to the nonconceptual. Any time we sit with an intention or hope of having some kind of experience, we are sitting with an "in order to," what Zen calls a "gaining idea." We are then in the separating function of the conceptual.

A Cree Indian medicine man I once knew told the following story: He and his fellow disciples once pressed the elder who was their teacher on what they needed to do to become awakened. "I can't tell you where to find a buffalo, but I *can* tell you it's not over there," the elder said to them, pointing to somewhere obvious, maybe the local gas station. By analogy we might say that we can't be told where or how to find oneness or suchness, but we can be told, "It's not over there"—namely, in the realm of the conceptual.

Partner or Group Exercises

Repeating questions: Ask (1) and (2) separately for 10 minutes each. No cross talk.

1. Tell me a way you have experienced oneness with something.
2. Ask (a), wait for answer, then ask (b), then back to (a), and so on.
    - a. Tell me a way you experience separation.
    - b. What is it like?

Monologue: 15 minutes each. No cross talk.

Continue inquiring into your experience of separation and oneness, even if it is retrospective. Consider the differences between actions that are automatic or habitual and those that are truly mindful. Also consider practicing mindfulness with actions that are normally automatic or habitual, such as brushing one's teeth. What would that be like?

Discuss together as long as you like.

12

Suchness, Uniqueness, and the Nonconceptual

"The total experience of a single thing" does not deprive a thing of its own unique particularity. It places a thing neither against others nor against none.
—DOGEN

"Not speaking" does not mean failing to express anything; for being able to express the truth is not the same as being able to speak.
—DOGEN

WHAT DO suchness, uniqueness, and the nonconceptual have to do with one other? To begin with, they are all aspects of oneness or nondual experience, also called "immediate" or "direct" experience. The best way to understand their connection to one another is through the important Buddhist concept and experience of emptiness.

To say that something is empty is to say that it has no "self-nature" or "inherent existence." This is true of any particular thing, as well as of the whole of reality, and can be deeply known experientially, though not with the everyday mind. One way to understand this is that nothing is *what* it is on its own. It can only be what it is through its comparing and contrasting connections to everything else, especially its nearby connections. In our everyday conceptual lives, this comparing and contrasting happens automatically and so fast we are not aware of it. When we know *what* something is, we know it is a this, not a that, which means it has borders, edges, boundaries. These boundaries are what allows it to be a this, not a that, and to have a concept or name with meaning.

Take the following example: A saucer isn't a saucer except through its connections to plate, cup, liquid, drink, and so forth. On Mars there might be objects that perfectly resemble our saucers, small disks with the circular indentations in which a cup could sit. But it turns out that on Mars there are no cups, no liquid, no drinking, and definitely no peeing. It might even be that the word Martians have for these small disks sounds like a guttural version of our word *saucer*. But without all the connections that give *saucer* its meaning, the Martian version, notwithstanding its perfect resemblance, wouldn't be anything like our saucers at all. Moreover, their word that sounds like *saucer* wouldn't mean the same as our word. Another way to say this is that the concepts are totally different. Perhaps the Martian saucer is a naturally occurring result of dust storms, and so in Martian it is not connected to concepts like *cup* and *tea* but rather *wind* and *dust*. Who knows, maybe on Mars there are no concepts of *wind* and *dust*, even though they have many of what we earthlings would call "dust storms." Because of their connections to different things, these identical-looking objects are not the same at all. Moreover, without their respective connections, the objects are experienced and understood to be empty. We experience the absence of conceptual connections in what Dogen calls "the total experience of a single thing." This is to experience something 100 percent. An example might be being totally absorbed in the book doing my homework. I no longer experience the book as a book as opposed to a pamphlet or notebook.

To know, at least intellectually, what suchness is, it is important to understand two things about emptiness. First, to say that something is empty is not to say it is like an empty vessel. In the Zen tradition, one of the most important aspects of something being empty is that, unlike an empty vessel, it has no sides, bottom, or top. This is why, as we've seen, in the experience of the emptiness of a particular thing, or even of the whole of reality, there can be no comparing or contrasting, no this-not-that, and thus no name or concept. The second most important thing about emptiness is surprising. Even though the experience of something as empty is nonconceptual, it nonetheless doesn't disappear or cease existing. We can still ask or be challenged to answer the question, "*What* is empty?" "Just this" can be the only answer. This is the suchness of whatever it is. Gestures and actions show up in many Zen exchanges between master and disciple, and they can also be an answer. As Dogen reminds us, "Being able to express the truth is not the same as being able to speak."[1]

Emptiness and suchness are the answers to two different questions about the same entity. Our everyday minds cannot make sense of this. How can something not be a "what,"

what Zen calls "no-thing," and at the same time be "just this?" The knowing here is prajna, knowing by being. Here is where Dogen tells us, "'The total experience of a single thing' does not deprive a thing of its own unique particularity. It places a thing neither against others nor against none."[2] Elsewhere Dogen says, "You should know that even though all things are liberated and not tied to anything, they abide in their own phenomenal expression."[3]

Not being "placed against others" or "tied to anything" means whatever it is, is not connected to anything; it is not a this or a that. We might make a koan out of this: How can something be a unique particular, a phenomenon, a form and yet have no boundaries?

Seeing the connection between emptiness and suchness, we can now look at the term *unique*. The experience of suchness is to experience something in its absolute particularity. This is not the same as experiencing a particular X as a particular version of such-and-such—like our saucer. Any saucer is a particular object that belongs to the category *saucer*, which contains many different kinds of saucer as well as many instances of the same kind. On the other hand, if we were to experience a particular saucer in its *uniqueness*—namely, in its *absolute* particularity—we would be experiencing its suchness. This, again, is what Dogen means by "the total experience of a single thing." When *uniqueness* is used in its original sense of being the only one, it has no predicates; there is no such thing as "unique in this or that respect." Nothing can be said about what is unique or absolutely particular.

One way suchness is described is to say that everything is "just as it is." Nothing is added—no stories, history, causes, analyses, comparisons, connections, categories, concepts, likes, or dislikes. As we've seen, Dogen says of anything experienced in its suchness that it is "not placed against" anything, as *saucer* is *saucer* only when placed against *cup* and a lot else. Another way he puts this is to say that anything experienced in its suchness is "a form beyond mutual opposition and dependence."[4] Of course, in order to conceptualize something is to place it in time in our vast knowledge and imagination of connections attained in the past or that could be attained in the future. But in the experience of the suchness of anything, "past and future are cut off."[5] Experiencing the suchness or the emptiness of anything is to experience the release of that thing or person from the separating boundaries of concepts—from its being this, not that; or its being a particular member of a general category. Dogen's word for this is "unstained." To experience "unstainedness" allows subject and object, whether persons or things, to be free to *interpenetrate* or to *be one with* one another, but without losing what Dogen, as we have seen, calls their own "unique particularity." But it isn't that I am here experiencing or "seeing" no boundaries in an objective something or someone over there, separate from me, in those moments. It is rather that I *am* that other, whatever or whoever it is. Whatever it is, is not an *object* of my awareness or knowing. It has become no-thing. I, too, as subject interpenetrating with that other, have become no-thing. Here is an example:

> Dongshan was once asked by a monastic, "When cold or heat comes, how can we avoid it?"
>
> Dongshan said, "Why don't you go to the place where there is no cold or heat?"
>
> The monastic said, "What is the place where there is no cold or heat?"
>
> Dongshan said, "When it is cold, let the cold kill you. When it is hot, let the heat kill you."[6]

It is not just the cold that is "killed" in this interpenetration but also the subject, the one who is cold.

One sure way to make something an object and hence conceptual is to prefer it or not prefer it to something else. "Faith in Mind" (Chinese, "Xinxin Ming"), the great poem of the Third Patriarch, Jianzhi Sengcan, of sixth-century China, famously begins with the line, "The Great Way is not difficult for those who have no preferences." It goes on to tell us, "When you grasp and reject, there is no suchness."[7] This release from conceptual boundaries is what the important Zen notion of *no obstruction* or *no hindrance* is about. When there are no conceptual boundaries, there is no obstruction to prevent interpenetration or oneness. Without obstruction or hindrance, both the subject and the object in their absolute particularity are totally free. Those of us used to chanting the *Heart Sutra* know the line "no hindrance, therefore no fear." As Dogen puts it in his fascicle "Bendowa" (On the Endeavor of the Way), "When we break through the barrier and drop off all limitations, we are no longer concerned with conceptual distinctions."[8]

In the case of the precepts, when I take stealing and not

stealing as opposites—or in other terms, when I am *pro*-not stealing and *anti*-stealing—I am creating conceptual boundaries around the precept. I am making them opposites that therefore obstruct or hinder each other. Can we let not stealing and especially stealing be *so themselves* that both they and I are killed? Being able to do this will get us to non-stealing.

13

A Defense of Concepts and Language

Not limited
By language,
It is ceaselessly expressed;
So, too, the way of letters
Can display but not exhaust it.
—DOGEN

BEFORE WE GO further in our exploration of nonduality and the precepts by delving into the topic of experience, there are some important points to make about language and the nonconceptual. First, animals are sometimes used as an example of what in the spiritual sense it would be to experience something in its nonconceptual "form," in the absolute now, or in its suchness. But animals exist in a preconceptual world, which would more appropriately be called "a-conceptual," whereas the spiritual experience of the nonconceptual is *post*-conceptual. Perhaps a clearer way to say this is that the adult human experience of the nonconceptual is the experience of a subject who lives in a highly conceptual world. It is the experience of something conceptual as nonconceptual—without name, without dependency and opposition. This is the nonduality of duality. Though the conceptual is often given a bad rap in Zen, everything we humans do and think or verbally express in our everyday world is conceptual. That is our distinctiveness, our greatness. It's what makes possible culture, history, and art, as well as conversation, breakfast, improvisation, riding a bicycle, driving a car, practicing with koans, and even the notion of "enlightenment."

Connected to this is the common idea in Buddhist circles that language is not only separate from reality but also somehow distorts it or acts as a veil between us and reality. One problem with this way of looking at it is that *reality* is itself a word. This view of language also comes with an assumption that, on the one hand, there is a separation between knower, thinker, or speaker, and "reality" on the other. This view treats language (and thought) as representational or purely descriptive and thus separate from what it is "about."

The irony in the mistake of thinking that Zen is somehow opposed to language is that the tradition is chock full of language! Its language, however, is not primarily representational but rather expressive and performative. An example of what philosophers mean by *performative* can be seen in promising. If I say, "I promised her yesterday that . . . ," I am using *promise* in a descriptive manner. It is then separate from what it is describing—namely, my promising yesterday. But when I say, "I promise . . . " in the first-person present tense, there is no separation: the promising is the words; the words are the promising. An example of this in the Zen tradition is the importance of vow, which shows up, among other places, at the end of the Jukai ceremony.

Not just vowing and promising but all of language—when heard, spoken, read, or written from a nondual place—is performative. Treating language as if it were just a finger pointing to the moon and not the moon itself makes it a means to an end and not an end in itself. This, for Dogen, would be like treating zazen as a means to an end outside of itself.

You may have noticed just above that I suggest hearing or listening can be a nondual experience. The Zen tradition is full of what are known as "turning words," words that trigger realization. A Zen student is expected to listen nondually to the words of the master in a talk or to read a sutra nondually. This means *just* listening or *just* reading—namely, doing so without any of the associations we automatically make in coming to understand something. As mentioned in the fourth precept, non-lying, like the New Testament's "those who have ears to hear," Dogen tells us, "If you are not willing to hear, the loudest voices could not reach your ears. If you are willing to hear, even the silent voices could reach your ears."[1] This, of course, is the point of the Zen story I mentioned in the introduction to part one. A monk who has heard the abbot say the same thing every day suddenly cries out with his tears falling, "Why haven't I heard this before?" This kind of hearing is a mystery to our everyday minds. Early in my Zen practice, occasionally tears would come when I heard the word *Absolute*, long before I had any experience of it. And then there is the Zen teaching "Everything preaches the Dharma." In truly coming to understand, experience, and live the nonduality of duality through our listening, reading, and perceiving in all realms of experience, we begin to see that that means we can experience and live the nonconceptuality of the conceptual. Another mystery best left as a mystery.

Dogen has quite a lot to say about language—much more than we can cover in this book on the precepts. Suffice it to say, he has strong criticisms of those who treat language, reason, and discrimination as somehow outside the Way. Here is his criticism of a "group of scatterbrained people" who mistakenly think that "only incomprehensible utterances are the talks of the Buddha ancestors":

> How pitiful are they who are unaware that discriminative thought *is* words and phrases and that words and phrases *liberate* discriminative thought![2]

After all, we discriminate between enlightenment and delusion, stealing and not stealing. and many other seeming opposites. The question is, can we do so using not the discrimination of our everyday minds but discriminating wisdom, so that they are realized as no longer opposites?

14

Experiencing Suchness

If you have immediacy,
immediacy is "dropping away"
with no obstacles.
—DOGEN

MUCH HAS been written about the nature of mystical experience and about whether Zen is a mysticism or not. In its Western history, the word *mystical* started out with a much narrower meaning than it has now. These days it is used for many different kinds of experience, including drug-induced ones, but this is not the place to go into all that. For our purposes, which include understanding oneness in relation to the precepts and why Hee-Jin Kim calls Dogen a "mystical realist," it is sufficient to call those experiences "mystical" that are nondual, nonconceptual glimpses of a reality not graspable by our everyday mind. You may recall from "The Three Levels of the Precepts" (p. 19) I once asked Cynthia Bourgeault why there are no so-called mystical experiences mentioned in the gospels, except for the Transfiguration, and she answered, "The mystic 'sees,' but that is different from 'living out of.'" In Zen this would be thought of as living one's realization. But instead of some general thing commonly called "actualization" in Zen, Dogen brings us face to face with knives, forks, friends, and precepts. Kim calls Dogen "a mystical realist" because he brings together the mystical—namely, the nondual—and the ordinary, everyday conceptual—namely, the dual—into a new "living out of." Let us consider what "seeing" and "living out of" are for Zen.

The "seeing" that is given so much importance in Zen is the nondual experience of the emptiness of the whole of reality or the Absolute, which includes the one having the experience. In that glimpse, what is experienced is utterly nonconceptual. This is both because it is a glimpse out of time and because it includes everything. There is no "outside," which means there is nothing to connect or compare it to, no "this, not that," and nobody to do the comparing. There is absolutely no way to describe it or the one experiencing herself as it. As a result, there is no more self-consciousness, that is, no more conceptualized object-self in the form of body or mind. The body-mind has "dropped off," to use Dogen's term for it. In one of his poems he says,

> If you have immediacy [oneness, nonduality]
> without defilement [concepts]
> immediacy is "dropping away" with no obstacles
> [borders, boundaries].[1]

Everything conceptual has dropped off.

As "The Identity of Relative and Absolute," an eighth-century Chinese Zen poem by Shitou Xiqian that is chanted daily in the Soto school, tells us, "To encounter the Absolute is not yet enlightenment."[2] What is also required for enlightenment is the return or rebirth of the relative—of the world as we know it, of life, of the self. This is sometimes described as a change of perspective about the self and the whole of reality, both of which are now, at least briefly, transformed. This involves, among other things, an end to the sense of separation. Zen has traditionally held that this kind of experience does not, as one might expect, represent the end point of practice but is actually the point at which it begins. This is the gradual, never-ending practice of actualization described by Master Hakuin, as mentioned in "The Three Levels of the Precepts." In my view, Dogen greatly deepens our understanding of this process.

Anything said about the experience of the whole of reality in Zen can be said about the experience of any of the particulars making it up. What Dogen helps us see is that, after what Zen calls "the Great Death," the rebirth of the world plunges us back into the temporal world of particulars—Dogen's world, our world—where no particular is excluded from Buddha-nature, not even a donkey's jaw, anxiety, or a broken wooden ladle.

In spite of the similarity that both the whole of reality and any given particular in that whole can be experienced nondually—and therefore nonconceptually—there is an important difference. The out-of-time glimpse of the whole of reality can *never* be conceptualized, whereas any particular in that whole not only *can* be but *is* conceptualized. Each particular, as we've seen, is a this, not a that, and is what it is because of its connections to other things. This includes thoughts, colors, emotions, small and large objects, people, breaths, tastes—everything. Each "this, not that" has a name and is a form. "Form" doesn't mean solid, separate, and permanent. It simply indicates the presence of borders and hence of conceptualizable objects of awareness. Ideas are forms. So are gases, precepts, and sensations, as well as material objects and other human beings.

Dogen describes the experience of a form as absolutely formless, absolutely nonconceptual, as an experience of its suddenly "leaping out" from a conceptual background. This means leaping out of time, and even leaping out of itself—namely, out of its conceptual what-it-is-ness. This leaping out is also described as a "leaping clear of the many and the one"[3]—namely, of the duality of relative and absolute. Such leaping clear allows us to experience that heaven and earth "co-exist eternally in each passing moment."[4] This is the identity of relative and absolute, the nonduality of duality.

The metaphor of "leaping out" is taken from a fish leaping out of water to get upstream to spawn. Like the fish, which has no resisting ground to push off from for its amazing leap, the leaping out of something in its suchness or nonconceptuality has nothing to "push off" from. The conceptual and the nonconceptual are in different categories; they are discontinuous. One can't lead to the other. There is an unbridgeable gap between the two. This is why the experience is sudden, like "an unexpected sneeze,"[5] coming from nowhere, and why it is an example of the samadhi of self-fulfilling activity, to be looked at in chapter 16.

Another of Dogen's terms for this is "total exertion." It's not just that we as subjects need to totally exert ourselves, but in doing so we allow a particular to totally exert itself.

Exertion is a misleading word here except when coupled with *total*. What exactly is total exertion? Martin Buber is helpful here: "An action of the whole being must approach passivity, for it does away with all partial actions and thus with any sense of action, which always depends on limited exertions."[6] When we totally exert ourselves, what I like to call "100 percent," there is nothing left over for self-consciousness or for "efforting." The passivity that is approached is absolute receptivity. Not only is there no sense of any "me" exerting itself but there is also no delusively "carrying myself forward," as Dogen puts it in "Genjō Kōan" (Actualizing the Fundamental Point), even ever so slightly in my perception of something or someone else. When I project absolutely nothing onto something else, it is allowed to reveal itself in its suchness, its absolute particularity, its nonconceptuality, its uniqueness. When the "leaping" happens, there is no self behind the perceiving and no object of the perceiving. There is just perceiving.

What about memory in relation to such experiences? That these experiences, these glimpses in the absolute now, happened, even when and where and of what, can be remembered, but their content cannot be remembered. Only the conceptual can be remembered. Here's an example: I remember a toaster "leaping out" during a silent retreat while I was waiting patiently for it to pop. When and where this happened, that it was a toaster and that I was very surprised, can be remembered. But if I try to remember the content of the experience, it becomes uncomfortably impossible. There is something there, but I cannot say, see, or know what. The *cannot* is not like an inability to make something out because of lack of enough light or being without my glasses. It is rather like the experience of a logical *cannot*, as in trying to imagine a square circle, only it's perceptual.

Even though we may not be aware of a "leaping out" experience in our everyday lives, we all know something of this in our experiences of suddenly understanding. We say, for instance, "It suddenly hit me that . . ." We also know it in getting a joke or bursting out laughing at something funny, in being struck by great beauty, in being moved to tears. Notice our language here: "bursting out," "being struck," " getting hit"—the passivity or receptivity of "being moved." It's as if in all these cases we were caught off guard and were totally open and receptive without even knowing it. In beginning to practice, we think we can bring out these moments if we only practice hard enough, but that would be "carrying ourselves forward," which is nothing but delusion. Dogen's way of saying that we can't bring about an experience of the nonconceptual is "Being unstained cannot be intended or discriminated at all."[7] Here is the unbridgeable gap again, the logical "cannot." We are like squares trying to imagine being circles without giving up our "squareness."

It sheds light on certain kinds of Zen experience to realize that after being "hit" or "struck," our minds go to the conceptual aftermath, which is the only place they *can* go. Our everyday minds are useless in glimpses out of time, of the suchness of a particular. As a result, we don't notice that those moments out of time teach us anything. We can appreciate and even say what was so funny, or beautiful, or shocking, or truly awesome, or what moved us. We realize and can say what we've suddenly understood. In these kinds of experiences, there is a certain momentary elation or, when trying hard to understand something, even relief. With certain spiritual experiences, we can describe the bliss, relief, or sense of freedom that follows. What we fail to notice in our everyday life experiences, unless it is pointed out, is the moment that preceded the temporal, conceptual aftermath. There was no subject or object in that moment. There was no-thing. What we also fail to notice is that the experience of the aftermath, at least briefly, is both nondual *and* conceptual. Even though I could explain the joke to someone who didn't get it, right after the moment of bursting out laughing, I do know what was so funny but it isn't all conceptually laid out and separate from me as an explanation would be. Here's an example of this in the experience of one of my students, Jamie Daikan Gemmiti, as he was working with one of the precepts:

> I had guests scheduled to arrive at my Airbnb on Thursday for the long Labor Day weekend. It's a very popular weekend in this resort area I'm in. The stay was going to bring in a good amount of money. During the overnight, Karen, my guest, wrote me a long email about the ordeal she and her husband just went through in tropical storm Ida in their hometown in New Jersey.
>
> They were trying to pick up their kids at work and they got stuck in high water and had to abandon their Chevy Suburban. She wrote they waded through waist-high water to get to safety and were

hoping they wouldn't have to evacuate their home at this point. She regretted she had to cancel their reservation.

It was shocking to read. Almost unbelievable, dream-like in that moment as I was waking up very early. My immediate thoughts and feelings were, embarrassingly, that I was glad they canceled late enough that they don't get a refund. I also thought maybe I could still rent it out and get a double payday.

During zazen soon after, it just hit me, as if the bottom fell out. I felt deeply what Karen and her family were going through in that moment. The fear and vulnerability was just palpable. I switched our zendo Zoom off immediately. I went on the Airbnb website and began to refund their money. I wrote a short note about how I could feel deeply their suffering and wanted them to know that I refunded all their money. Karen wrote back that she cried when she read my email and was grateful for my note and the refund.

You can see here that something "leapt out" at my student—he didn't intend or expect to have this realization, though having worked through allowing the liar, stealer, stingy one, and so on in himself many times before made it more likely for such an experience to occur.

Let's return to the example of the toaster that "leapt out" during my retreat: after the experience of the out-of-time glimpse of the absolute formlessness of a form or a particular, we return to what we might call the relative formlessness of a form or particular. The toaster is *just* a toaster. We can let it be just as it is. Eventually we return to its separating, boundaried conceptualization, but with more and more practice and experience, our world begins to change. We start "living out of" our realization more and more, which means experiencing things, people, and precepts more often just as they are with no added stories, expectations, reactions, shoulds, preferences, or concepts. We start experiencing less separation, and at the same time a kind of spaciousness and freedom in our form-filled world. This is what Dogen calls "coming from the side of Buddha" in the relative world of functioning. Functioning includes all that we do, even perceiving and thinking:

> When you let go of both your body and mind,
> forget them both
> and throw yourself into the house of Buddha,
> and when the functioning
> begins from the side of Buddha drawing you in
> to accord with it,
> then, with no need of any expenditure of either
> physical or mental
> effort, you are freed from birth-and-death and
> become Buddha. There can be no obstacle in
> anyone's mind.[8]

When "functioning begins from the side of Buddha," this is the nonduality of duality. In his works on Dogen, Hee-Jin Kim calls our temporal, ever-changing, beautiful, and difficult world in these nondual moments "revisioned." In

Dogen's mystical realism, the world of duality in which we live is not transcended but it is rather, in other of Kim's words, "revalorized," "redeemed," "liberated," "revaluated," "authenticated," "reconstituted," and "realized."[9] And because reality is an ever-changing dynamism, and because our "vast and giddy karmic consciousness" is never-ending, the realization and redemption happen over and over again. This is practice. This is where stealing and not stealing both cease being conceptually bounded, are realized as empty, known in their suchness, and thus are liberated into non-stealing.

15

The Suchness of the Subject

If you wish to attain suchness, you should practice suchness without delay.
—DOGEN

The appearance of the self which is beyond speech.
—DOGEN

SO FAR, we've considered the suchness of the object in the experience of oneness with a particular, but this includes the suchness of the subject as well. Otherwise, who would be doing the "one with?" As we've seen, *penetration* is a Zen word, important to Dogen, for the experience of the suchness of a particular. But in Zen's urging us as practitioners, as subjects, to experience the suchness of something, to penetrate it, to be one with it, to experience immediacy with it, we forget that penetration is not one-sided and that what is required is *interpenetration.* Interpenetration is mutual nonconceptuality or boundarylessness, hence, freedom from hindrance or obstruction for both subject and object. Dogen reminds us of this in the following way: "Only when one encounters things penetratingly is one genuinely free in the very act of encountering."[1]

One way of saying what happens to the object of awareness of knowing in this kind of experience is that it is no longer "objectified." It has become what Zen calls "no-thing." But as Dogen reminds us in his *Shōbōgenzō* fascicle "Gabyo" (The Pictured Cakes), it doesn't lose "its own unique particularity." In our everyday dualistic experience, on the other hand, we not only objectify objects but also subjects, namely, ourselves. Experiencing ourselves as objects is self-consciousness—precisely that which Zen hopes to free us of. As we've seen in the chapter on the first precept, non-killing, this is what Master Yunmen calls "sitting with a sit-view" and "walking with a walk-view." It involves bifurcating ourselves into two—a subject, *I*, and an object, *me*. *I*, as subject, am aware of conceptualizable *me*—namely, all my mental, physical, and emotional characteristics. This *me* is what we all know in the ordinary sense of knowing. But what if we also try to know the *I* in this ordinary, separating way of knowing? It's as if another I pops up and is aware of the first I, now an object. I have turned the original I into a *me*, and on ad infinitum.

What exactly is this *I*? What is revealed on close inspection is that the *I* is never conceptualizable and can never be an object. The only way to know the *I* is to *be* it 100 percent and this, as we've seen, is no subject-object knowing. When I am 100 percent myself, there is no self-consciousness. I am I, no longer bifurcated into an I and a me. When this happens, the body-mind—namely, the conceptualizable object *me* that I think I am—"drops off." This 100 percent being myself is very important for many things we intentionally do, like skiing down a dangerous slope. But it also occurs unexpectedly in emergencies, suddenly understanding something, and many other examples, mentioned in the preceding chapter. There is no *me* in these moments.

In my example in chapter 11 of being one with reading a book in the library and losing all sense of separation and conceptualization, things nonetheless don't lose their "unique particularity," as Dogen tells us. In this state, I take another sip from the coffee mug and don't attempt to take it from the pen on the desk. What about the unique particularity of the subject? We are each of us unique.

Kodo Roshi tells us that we cannot exchange even a fart with someone else. Again, think about that word *unique.* As noted before, in its original use, it has no predicates. Whatever is unique can't be better or worse than anything else. But more importantly, it can't even be this, not that—woman, not man; blond, not brunette; human being as opposed to squirrel; sentient as opposed to non-sentient; this particular life history as opposed to that one. Our delusions that we are solid, separate, and permanent all involve the "this as opposed to that" comparing. The classic Buddhist delusions behind all these more psychological comparisons are that we are solid as opposed to transparent; permanent as opposed to impermanent; separate as opposed to not separate. Anything that is unique in the primary sense of this word is free of all comparisons and is thus *absolutely particular*—and this includes the subject that we are in addition to the objects we are aware of.

To be *absolutely* particular is not to be the particular of a general, like the species of a genus or an individual representative of a species. Anything that is absolutely particular cannot be compared to anything and hence it cannot be described. It is empty. What is empty? *Me*, a person of suchness—*just this*. Finally, just an I, which means nothing to be described or attached to, nothing to be promoted or protected. Finally free. But from the point of view of everyday mind, the idea of this state can be a little scary. After all, who wants to be nobody? Eventually, however, those of us who begin a practice like Zen see how the somebody we think we are is the source of our inability to live with an ease of being.

Let's apply all this to the precept of non-stealing. Where there is a me to be aware of, I am aware of myself as not stealing and as having successfully observed a precept. The "I" is separately and approvingly observing the "me" not stealing. Moreover, I feel good about being good. From the point of view of everyday mind, it is hard to imagine not stealing without any self-consciousness, without a me, without a should. But as Dogen tells us, the more we practice suchness, the more we will become a person of suchness. How do we do that?

In his fascicle "Fukanzazengi" (Universal Promotion of the Principles of Zazen), Dogen tells us if we want to be a person of suchness, we need to practice suchness right away. The fundamental practice of suchness for Dogen is zazen, or more particularly, shikantaza, "just sitting." The "just" here is "nothing else but." Having our sitting practice reveal itself as suchness is to experience it without its being connected to anything else. Of course, we know that means we are just sitting and not following thoughts, feelings, and so forth. But we have to remember that sitting could also be conceptually "connected to" walking, standing, or lying down if we were to take the experience of the sitting posture *as opposed to* those. It could also be connected to a goal, a reason, a why-am-I-doing-this—connected, that is, to something outside itself, like seeking to become a buddha. But to be truly zazen, the enactment of enlightenment, there is nothing but it. It is empty of self-nature. It is "just this." It has no borders and yet doesn't lose its absolute particularity. It can interpenetrate with anything or everything, and occasionally in sitting, the universe interpenetrates with it. This is the person of suchness engaging in the practice of suchness. The perfect freedom of *just sitting*.

And as we've seen, it is of this state of zazen—of being a person of suchness practicing suchness—that Dogen says, "What precept is not followed?" This is the perfect freedom of non-stealing.

16

The Samadhi of Self-Fulfilling Activity

The Buddhas and Tathagatas have an excellent way—unequalled and natural—to transmit the wondrous Dharma through personal encounter and to realize supreme enlightenment. As it is imparted impeccably from Buddha to Buddha, its criterion is the samadhi of self-fulfilling activity [*jijuyu sammai*]. For playing joyfully in such a samadhi the upright sitting position in meditation is the right gate.
—DOGEN

TO CALL an activity "self-fulfilling"—whether it's just sitting, just eating, just jogging, or just voting—is to say it is self-sufficient, not dependent on anything else. It is free of reasons, grounds, goals, or outcomes.

Play is the best example of something that is always self-fulfilling. In fact, Zen has a term for the "samadhi of play" (*yuge sammai*). Games have rules and are played in order to be won, whether or not that is the intention of the players. The "goal" of play, on the other hand, is play itself. There is no goal outside of play. When shikantaza, just sitting, can be just as it is, it is self-fulfilling. In those moments it is absolutely particular. It is unique. I am it, just as when I am completely absorbed reading a book in the library and there is no longer a "me." This is what Dogen calls "the appearance of self which is beyond speech."[1] Everything objective and hence conceptual has "dropped off." And as he teaches us in "Genjō Kōan" (Actualizing the Fundamental Point), when my body-mind drops off, the body-mind of everything else drops off as well. There is nothing outside the subject on which to depend, aim for, or be compared to. These self-fulfilling moments are the essence of freedom, spontaneity, and creativity. We are empty, unique, and without boundaries and thus can freely interpenetrate with another, with a precept, with particular circumstances.

I have heard the Advaita teacher Francis Lucille call a groundless, purposeless, self-fulfilling action "a celebration." Dogen says of shikantaza, "The zazen I speak of is not learning meditation practice. It is simply the Dharma gate of peace and bliss, the practice-realization of totally culminated awakening. It is things as they are in suchness."[2] Commenting on this teaching, the Zen teacher and translator Taigen Dan Leighton says, "Dogen's zazen is a ritual expression and celebration of awakening already present."[3] It is expression not in the sense of something there waiting to be expressed. The awakening *is* the expression. The expression *is* the awakening. This becomes important in understanding what "becoming" a buddha means in the context of the Jukai ceremony, which we will look at further on. Francis Lucille's sense of celebration is not in the sense of something already there to be celebrated, which is, indeed, a way the word is ordinarily read. It is rather "cut off from before and after," the self-fulfilling joy or bliss of true spontaneity. Spontaneity is too often associated with noise and fun. The spontaneity associated with Zen is simply a groundless samadhi of self-fulfilling activity.

The fish leaping into the air is the perfect example of a self-fulfilling activity. A fish leaping into the air has nothing to push off from. It is completely self-sufficient. It's like an absolute autonomy. It's amazing to discover that it isn't just us subjects who can experience that. Everything in the universe, including the universe as a whole, when it is coming from the side of Buddha, is, in its being and doing, self-fulfilling. And that includes each precept.

Partner or Group Exercises

Repeating questions: Ask (1) and (2) separately for 10 minutes each. No cross talk.

1. Tell me a way you are self-conscious.
2. Tell me a moment your self-consciousness "dropped off."

Monologue: 15 minutes each. No cross talk.

Reflect back on moments of true spontaneity and notice the "self-fulfilling" nature of whatever is occurring.

Discuss together as long as you like.

17

Oneness of Self and Other

Great enlightenment right at this moment is not self, not other.

—DOGEN

Identity with others is nondifference. This applies equally to the self and to others. . . . As we understand identity with others, self and others are one indivisible suchness. . . . There is a truth that after self assimilates others to itself, self lets itself be assimilated by others. The relationship of self and others is infinitely [varied] according to circumstances.

—DOGEN

WHAT KIND of separation and oneness do we experience with other people? Of course, any kind of reactivity is a dead giveaway that separation is occurring. Think about the experience of a sense of "I'm here, and you—you're over there." Or "I'm this way, not that way." Or worse, as first mentioned in the discussion of the sixth precept, non-talking about others' errors and faults, "Thank God, I don't have her elbows." All our self-images, judgments, insecurities, self-protections, self-promotions, and most of our fears are created by and continue to create separation.

Every single one of the precepts addresses our separation from others. Take stealing: You have something I want or think I need. You, me, and the something you have all appear as bordered, separate forms. Separation is the main source of our own suffering and certainly the source of our causing suffering in others.

What would oneness with others be like? Bernie Glassman used to demonstrate oneness in the realm of manyness by imagining the absurdity of my right hand hesitating to put out the flames burning my left hand, or my right hand stealing or refraining from stealing from my left hand as my left hand reaches for money being handed to it. It makes no sense. As I write this, another hurricane is approaching the Caribbean. Houston was completely flooded, several islands flattened, and Puerto Rico totally devastated. On the news, when we see human beings rushing to the aid of other human beings as well as rescuing animals, we are often deeply moved. This kind of reaction from the outside makes sense, but those rushing to the aid of others are often simply experiencing what is meant by natural and spontaneous expression of the precepts. They are no longer moral principles separate from us. They are, in a sense, our very being—and so are other people, dogs, cats, cows, and trees. Others, then, are like my left hand, and I am like my right hand automatically, spontaneously putting out the fire. All of reality is then One Body.

It's important to find experiences like this in our own lives, perhaps as dramatic as grabbing a child who is about to run into the street, or as subtle as just truly listening to someone else. Dogen calls this being "unstained" or "undefiled" and uses the example of "meeting a person and not considering what he looks like"—or what he said to me last week, what his politics are, and so forth.[1] "Unstained" is not dependent (as the concept *saucer* is dependent on *cup*) or opposed (the concept *short* is opposed to *tall*). His notion of something being unstained is like our notion of nonconceptual. And it is similar to Martin Buber's "you" in the I-you relation. Unlike the "it" (which includes he, she, they, we) in the I-it relation, the you, in Buber's language, is "neighborless and seamless."[2] Truly speaking to or listening to another, truly saying "you" to that other, is experiencing the other as a formless form, as suchness.

Those in our No Traces Sangha who have done the precept exercises as well as similar exercises with other Zen teachings have reported experiencing moments of oneness with their partners. What happens is that our natural self-protection in being asked to reveal what we'd rather keep hidden, even from ourselves, eventually gives way to compassionate allowing. The heart opens not just to the other but also to our own shame or fear that someone else can know about my stealing, lying, or sexual misconduct. For a moment the borders fall away. This is Dogen's body-mind "dropping off."

What drops off is the conceptual.

Partner or Group Exercises

Repeating questions: Ask (1) and (2) separately for 10 minutes each. No cross talk.

1. Tell me a way you experience separation from others.
2. Tell me a way you experience oneness with others.

Monologue: 15 minutes each. No cross talk.

Reflect on in which situations you experience separation and in which you experience oneness.

Discuss together as long as you like.

18

Oneness and the Way of the Bodhisattva

The Way of the Bodhisattva is I am suchness,
you are suchness.
—DOGEN

BERNIE GLASSMAN always said that the bodhisattva does "what is needed." Her response is like answering the call of one's name—direct, immediate, spontaneous, nondual. As noted in the previous chapter, human beings tend to respond in just this way in wars and natural disaster emergencies. During the horrible shooting that took place in a New Zealand mosque in 2019, a woman drove into the parking lot just as two men, who had both been shot, came stumbling toward her. She didn't turn her car around to get away. She stopped the car and dragged one of the men into the car, where she worked hard to stop the bleeding. Here's a Bloomberg News description of what happened afterward:

> Her voice cracking, she went on, "In the meantime, the poor guy across the road passed away." She paused. "I never thought in my life I would live to

> see something like this. Not in New Zealand." The reporter tried to console her. "We really commend you for what you did. You're really a hero." "No, I'm not," she said. "No, you just do what you do at the time. I wish I could've done more."[1]

This is the way of the bodhisattva. No separation here—no stories, no choices, no should. Nothing conceptual about the object, the subject, or the circumstances. No boundaries, hence nothing to hinder or obstruct oneness. Notice also that the "voice cracking" occurs afterward in the retelling. Often one hears exactly the response of this woman when what we like to think of as "heroism" is praised as such. Her conceptualized self as an object, hero or not hero, was not there while she was saving the life of a man who had been shot. The possibility of this borderlessness is why we can be "one with" anything, knowing whatever it is from the inside by being it—and also being known by it from the inside. I can't know the other as suchness unless I am suchness myself. The following koan expresses this:

> Caoshan asked Senior Monastic De, "Buddha's true Dharma body is like empty sky. It reflects forms just like water. How do you express this principle?"
>
> De said, "It's like a donkey looking at a well."
>
> Caoshan said, "You have got the point, but you have said only eighty or ninety percent of it."
>
> De said, "Master, how would you say it?"
>
> Caoshan said, "It's just like a well looking at the donkey."

Capping Verse

When the teacher sees the student,
  the student sees the teacher.
For the student to meet the teacher,
  he must be the teacher.
Isn't this the teacher meeting herself?
Isn't this the student meeting himself?[2]

Dogen's "Genjō Kōan" (Actualizing the Fundamental Point) puts this in a slightly different way: "To carry yourself forward and experience myriad things is delusion. That myriad things come forth and experience themselves is awakening."[3] This awakening comes from our complete allowing of anything to be "just as it is" without any binding concepts, stories, or descriptions. In the case of the interpersonal, this is "I am suchness, you are suchness"—the way of the bodhisattva. To stick with the non-stealing precept, when I am suchness and you are suchness, there are no hindrances, no separation, so it makes no sense for me to experience myself as lacking anything or to experience you as having something I want. There is no you and no me. There is just "self and others in one indivisible suchness."[4] And yet the situation is such that stealing as opposed to blaming could take place. The precepts don't disappear in one indivisible suchness—it's just that they are no longer precepts in any conventional, conceptual sense.

Partner or Group Exercises

Repeating questions: Ask (1) and (2) separately for 10 minutes each. No cross talk.

1. Tell me a way you have, like the bodhisattva, done precisely what was needed without separation or self-consciousness.
2. Tell me a way you have failed to do precisely what was needed.

Monologue: 15 minutes each. No cross talk.
Reflect on this.

Discuss together as long as you like.

19

Opening

Concentration without elimination.

—T. S. ELIOT

Total exertion of a single thing.

—DOGEN

HOW DO we become bodhisattvas? How do we open to the possibility of oneness—with the other? Certain of Dogen's remarks make it seem as if concentration, rather than openness, is what is needed. For instance, he writes, "if my self does not put forth the utmost exertion and live time now, not a single thing will be realized."[1] Also, "If you concentrate your effort single-mindedly, you are thereby negotiating the Way with your practice-realization undefiled." But we need to be cautious about how we understand the word *concentration*. It is here that T. S. Eliot's three words from the *Four Quartets*—"Concentration without elimination"—are invaluable. I've always thought that these three words should be at the heart of every beginning meditation instruction.

So often, in beginning to practice zazen by concentrating on something like counting exhalations, or even on just sitting, the meditator assumes that she needs somehow to push away whatever becomes distracting. That, of course, is like pouring kerosene on fire, not to mention that it is turning our attention away from whatever it is we are to stay with 100 percent, namely, from the single thing we are to experience ourselves as being—breath, numbers, koan, or just sitting. Kodo Roshi defines the *shikan* in *shikantaza* (just sitting) as "not turning away." This is the meaning of the "just" in "just sitting." It means "only sitting," or "not turning away" from it by getting on trains of thought or trying to push away distractions. But, again, not turning away from something is not the same as eliminating or excluding everything else. That would be another turning way. Moreover, excluding anything is to create boundaries that discriminate the excluded from the included. Doing that puts us back in the realm of the conceptual, the this as opposed to that, container thinking, the realm of boundaries and obstruction or hindrance.

Dogen mentions two other ways that we turn away from what we are to be with 100 percent. One is that we sit with an "in order to," an intention to gain something—say, to relieve some suffering, become a better version of myself, or even become a buddha. Then sitting is no longer a self-fulfilling samadhi. Kodo Roshi reminds us that "we don't eat in order to take a shit, and we don't shit in order to make manure."[2] Perhaps the Zen Peacemakers' first tenet, Not Knowing, is what we need here, as it points to a total openness. Not knowing in this sense is a state of nonconceptualizing. Let's revisit Dogen's term "unstained," sometimes translated as "undefiled," to inquire further. Dogen has raised the question of what it is like to be unstained, and he responds:

> To be unstained does not mean that you try forcefully to exclude intention or discrimination, or that you establish a state of nonintention. Being unstained cannot be intended or discriminated at all.
>
> Being unstained is like meeting a person and not considering what he looks like. Also it is like not wishing for more color or brightness when viewing flowers or the moon.
>
> Spring has the tone of spring, and autumn has the scene of autumn; there is no escaping it. So when you want spring or autumn to be different from what it is, notice that it can only be as it is. Or when you want to keep spring or autumn as it is, reflect that it has no unchanging nature.
>
> . . . When you clarify that there is nothing to be disliked or longed for, then the original face is revealed by your practice of the way.[3]

"Forcefully to exclude intention or discrimination" is just another intention and discrimination. To try to "establish a state of nonintention" is just another intention. Since we can't bring about the state of unstainedness, which would be an example of "carrying the self forward," Dogen suggests that we, at least, reflect on the delusion of permanence and "clarify that there is nothing to be disliked or longed for." We usually think of reflecting and clarifying in conceptual terms, but in this context it means careful 100 percent openness. This is also what happens in the practice of allowing, even welcoming, the killer, liar, and stealer in us in the presence of another. We start experiencing these parts of ourselves as "unstained," which means we experience them as nonconceptual, not the opposite of anything. This, as we will see, is key in moving from not to non.

A useful term here for the wide-open, receptive state we have to be in is *choiceless awareness.* "Meeting a person and not considering what he looks like" or "not wishing for more color" is to be free of comparing, free of this as opposed to that. It is, as "Faith in Mind" puts it, to be free of preferences, and in that to discover that "the Great Way is not difficult." It is to stop what Dogen calls "binding one's self without a rope"[4]—namely, binding ourselves conceptually and thus experiencing ourselves as separate from everything else. Again, to use Bernie's three Zen Peacemaker tenets, if we can be in a state of *not knowing*—that is, totally open—then we can *bear witness to* whatever arises. Bearing witness means letting things "take their course," or in another translation, "be as they are," as "Faith In Mind" puts it. If we can truly do that, we will be granting freedom to whatever is unfolding, including to the killer, liar, stealer in me. As Dogen puts it in his "Fukanzazengi,"

> You should therefore cease from practice based on intellectual understanding, pursuing words and following after speech, and learn the backward step that turns your light inward to illuminate yourself. Body and mind will drop away of themselves, and your original face will manifest itself. If you wish to

> attain suchness, you should practice suchness without delay. . . . The zazen I speak of is not learning meditation. It is simply the Dharma-gate of repose and bliss. It is the practice-realization of totally culminated enlightenment. It is things as they are in suchness.[5]

This is the practice of total openness.

Partner or Group Exercises

Monologue: 15 minutes each. No cross talk.

Reflect on your experiences of opening to something you were once closed to.

Discuss together as long as you like.

20

Oneness and Compassion

Please call me by my true names,
so I can wake up
and the door of my heart
could be left open,
the door of compassion.
—THICH NHAT HANH

All buddhas' compassion and sympathy for sentient beings are neither for their own sake nor for others.
—DOGEN

WHAT DO oneness and compassion have to do with one another? It might seem that compassion requires separation, and given a certain understanding of compassion, that is true. You're over there, you're you, and you're suffering something or other. I'm over here, I'm me, and I'm able empathically to feel your feelings without identifying with you. This means that there is enough distance to enable me to feel your feelings without completely identifying with you—without, as we say, drowning with the drowning man. This kind of compassion could be termed *feeling-compassion*. It's where my acting to relieve your suffering is based on my ability and maybe desire to feel your feelings and connect them to my own.

The compassion of the bodhisattva who spontaneously does what is needed is different in that it is not based on feeling. It's not based on anything. It is self-fulfilling! My left hand is burning, so my right hand puts out the fire without being motivated by feelings or precepts or anything else. It is automatic, spontaneous, natural. This is the compassion of oneness. It is intrinsic to oneness. It *is* oneness. The woman in New Zealand jumping out of her car and dragging the man bleeding to death into her car to stop his bleeding, as mentioned in chapter 18, was not feeling his feelings and then acting on them. She was him. There is no space for shoulds or oughts in that expression of compassion. He was like her burning hand. This kind of behavior is nondual, nonconceptual. We might say it is the suchness of compassion. As quoted as the epigraph to chapter 18, Dogen says it in the following way: "The Way of the Bodhisattva is 'I am suchness. You are suchness.'"[1]

This compassion shows up not just in our relation to others. It is the compassion intrinsic to our allowing, even welcoming, the various forms of precept-breaker in us. Perhaps, at first, I am separate from, in the sense of hiding or rejecting, some part of myself—say, the one who lies and hides it. It might be shame or fear that prevents me from acknowledging to myself and then to others that liar in me. Getting closer to welcoming it—maybe into my living room, to use a silly metaphor—is an act of compassion usually based on feeling. But the closer we get to it, maybe now inviting it to sit on the same couch with me, allows a kind of compassionate curiosity to begin to take the place of shame and fear. And then it can happen that I slowly but surely move to the end of the couch where the rejected part is sitting. I am so close to it I no longer know its name. It has no name. And neither do I. Here is where it is released from all the connections that give it its name and make it conceptual. I become one with it. I *am* it.

In the case of something like anger, which, unlike the others, is a precept about an emotion, we might say that in that oneness its energy is liberated from its conceptual barriers and confines. Psychospiritually, a kind of Tantric transformation can take place so that, as the Tibetan Buddha families show us, the "poison" of anger is transmuted into the "medicine" of clarity. The clarity here, however, is not in the same realm or category as anger. It cannot, therefore, be the opposite of anger—or the opposite of anything else; for example, lack of clarity. There are many different terms for the negative emotions thought of as poisons in Tibetan Buddhism—*confusions*, *afflictions*, *defilements*—but what I like to think of as the "liberated" versions of the energy involved are all thought of as *wisdoms*. They are not just the good versions of negative or egoic emotions. They have no opposites and hence no borders. They are suchness. They are self-fulfilling.

Oneness of Subject and Rejected Parts of the Self

We have now looked at separation and oneness as they apply to several topics—subject and object, self and other, language and activity. From the standpoint of precept practice, one of the most important inquiries concerning separation and oneness has to do with those parts of ourselves that we are tempted to reject, deny, or hide. Usually we reject or deny parts of ourselves because they don't fit a self-image we have, a way we would like to be seen. We could think of this as due to either self-protection or self-promotion. Sometimes it's fear that causes the rejection. Practicing with the precepts by really seeing and allowing the killer, liar, stealer, and so forth in us is, again to borrow Dogen's phrasing, to "clarify that there is nothing to be disliked or longed for."[2] It is what he would call an "unstained" relationship with these parts of ourselves. This is the crucial first step in opening to oneness with the Zen precepts. It is a profoundly compassionate practice. It is also a necessary practice, because it is only compassion for ourselves that allows us to have compassion for others.

Thich Nhat Hanh's famous poem "Please Call Me by My True Names," which I included in the discussion of the seventh precept, is about our being one with the other, whether that other is a flower, a frog, an arms merchant, or a rapist. When I find the idea of being one with a flower or someone I admire or love easier than being one with an arms merchant or a rapist—or a frog—then I can be sure there is something I reject in myself. There are, then, boundaries, concepts, objects. As mentioned in the chapter on non-talking about others' errors and faults, the Roman playwright Terence reminds us, "Nothing human is foreign to me."

The second step is to get so close to whatever it is that I no longer know its name. It's no longer a this as opposed to a that. It's not "I am a liar as opposed to a truth-teller." If I can allow myself to be 100 percent the liar that I am, it ceases to be conceptual, ceases to have boundaries, and thus ceases to be something to resist—like the cold that is killed in the story about Dongshan and his monk (p. 152). I and it become the oneness of suchness. There is nothing left to reject. As Dogen explained in the introduction to part one, "When a demon becomes a buddha, it exerts its demoness, breaks it, and actualizes a buddha."[3] When a liar becomes a buddha, she exerts her lying, breaks it, and actualizes a buddha.

Partner or Group Exercises

Repeating questions: Ask (1) and (2) separately for 10 minutes each. No cross talk.

1. Tell me a way you opened with compassionate allowing to something in yourself.
2. Tell me something that was difficult to compassionately allow and disclose to another.

Monologue: 15 minutes each. No cross talk.

Reflect on these two questions.

Discuss together as long as you like.

21

Oneness and the Precepts

There is no delusion that obstructs great enlightenment.

—DOGEN

HAVING NOW COVERED a number of topics related to oneness, suchness, and compassion, I hope you have begun to sense what it could mean to be one with a precept. All we have to do is to notice our language here. There are many different words, in both secular and religious contexts, used for ethical precepts—*principles, injunctions, rules for proper conduct, commandments, prohibitions, norms, standards,* and still more. In all these cases, the precept or principle is treated as in some sense outside of us, separate from us, and is used as a standard or guide for proper conduct, telling us what we should and should not do. That separation can be seen in the language we use for our relation to precepts—*follow, keep, adhere to,* or *observe.*

Something like the Three Pure Precepts and the Ten Grave Precepts of Zen can be found in every religious tradition or path. Something like them is also to be found as secular ethical principles or norms of behavior in every culture. Such precepts or principles can always be related to in three distinct ways. When precepts are taken in either the absolutist, "never-ever" sense or in the relative-to-context sense, we have some version of a dualistic relation to them, as described above. In the third, nondual way of taking the precepts, to be found in Western mystical traditions and in the Dogen Zen we are considering here, they have in a certain sense ceased being precepts. We are in the realm of no separation and therefore are one with the precepts.

It may be helpful here to consider the following analogy: Imagine you are part of a dance group, and the choreographer has come up with a new dance and written down its choreography. You have its score, and while holding it in your hands, you use it to help you go through the proper motions in relation to the other dancers and the music. The score—and, especially at first, the choreographed moves it calls for—are separate from you. Eventually you are able to internalize the score and carry it around in your head, to be mentally consulted when needed. It's still separate. Finally, you are one with it, and the dance happens automatically. If you penetrate it even further, there are likely to be moments when the dance not only happens spontaneously but seems to come from a place where there is no dancer, no doer, no "me," and even no dance. The dance goes on, but it is no longer conceptualized and thus no longer something a describable "me" is doing. Each dancing moment is free of past and future, and free in all senses from the question "Why?" As in "Why are you doing it this way?" The answer is no longer "Because the choreography says to do it this way" but rather "I just am."

According to Zen, this type of transformation can occur in all aspects of life, including with the precepts. I suspect that all of us have had the experience of naturally or spontaneously expressing the heart of one of the precepts without the separation of a "Should I?" or "Shouldn't I?" and without a "Why?" The question "Why?" only makes sense when there is separation between the one who acts and the precept. In those cases, there is an answer such as "Because it is the right thing to do." Neither my student mentioned in chapter 14 nor the New Zealand woman mentioned in chapter 18 were functioning with a "Why?" and a "Because it was the right thing to do."

Perhaps we can now understand in a new light Dogen's teaching, "When we sit zazen, what precept is not observed, what merit is not actualized?"[1] As noted above, for Dogen, zazen, or sitting meditation, is not a means to the end of enlightenment but rather an expression of enlightenment. Like a face and its expression, they are one. At this stage, the precepts, which are intrinsic to enlightenment and not the result of enlightenment, arise naturally and spontaneously. We are one with them, having left the realm of the conceptual and entered the realm of suchness. We are their embodied manifestation. It is here that it only makes sense to use *non* instead of *not* or *don't*.

At this point we can ask, how do we get there with the precepts? Here the Zen practice of no preferences is valuable. This is what the practices with the precepts in part one are all about. Can I so deeply allow the killer or the liar in me that I cease the pattern of attachment and rejection by making them opposites of the exclusionary "not" version of each precept?

One way for us to understand the use of *non* instead of

not with each of the Zen precepts is to remind ourselves again of Master Sengcan's poem "Faith in Mind," in which he writes, "The Great Way is not difficult for those who have no preferences." The preferences meant here—liking and disliking, grasping and rejecting—are due to comparing mind, to setting up better against worse. In order to do that, as we've seen, we have self-consciously to take something to be a "this" as opposed to a "that" with a slight element of preference. This is the beginning of separation. On first reading the beginning of the poem, many people mistakenly think it's prohibiting preferences so that I can no longer prefer vanilla ice cream to chocolate—or not lying to lying. That is not at all what is meant here. It is rather the attachment to one thing and rejection of another or many others that is being addressed. It's the same with other people, too. I can definitely prefer my candidate to yours, or the company of one person over another, but can I do so without attachment and rejection? Can I be aware of my preference or opinion without creating polarization? I am separate when I am one pole of a polarization—they are Republicans and *I am definitely not one of those!* But I am also separate when I treat things or persons as opposed to one another in a polarized sense—Republicans and Democrats are mutually exclusive, definitely not free to interpenetrate. As Dogen reminds us, we mistakenly do that with delusion and enlightenment, and this is the meaning of "There is no delusion that obstructs great enlightenment."[2] Delusion and enlightenment are *nonopposed.* When I treat things as mutually exclusive, I exclude myself from them, I become separate from them. "[This] is like binding oneself without a rope."[3] Not only do I become bound "without a rope," but so do they. Everything is then boundaried and obstructing everything else.

It is the same with the precepts. I can be attached to *should-not-steal* and reject *stealing*. Right there I am creating a dualism of opposites, a polarization. I can never then be one with a precept. Moreover, this attachment to "should" and "should not" can, of course, make us powerfully judgmental. I remember as a ten-year-old child going with my two-years-younger brother and our four-year-old sister to Woolworths to get something for our mother. We told our sister to stay by the candy counter while we went searching for whatever we were supposed to get. We got back to her and were all set to return home, but she couldn't move for some reason. We noticed one arm behind her back. It turned out she had stuck her hand into a small opening in the glass cover and was holding a fistful of candy. The opening was too small for her fist, but not for her hand. She would have to let go of the candy, and she refused to do so. Once we finally got her to let go of the candy, we two older know-it-all siblings were perfectly horrible to her, accusing her of stealing without any letup all the way home. Given the way we treated her, you'd think she had been guilty of embezzling money from an organization designed to help the poor! My brother's and my relation to the temptation to steal—both our own and other people's—was clearly in the polarizing "not" category.

Partner or Group Exercises

Repeating questions: Ask (1) and (2) separately for 10 minutes each. No cross talk.

1. Tell me a way you have felt a "should" with one of the precepts.
2. Tell me a way you have felt a "should not" with one of the precepts.

Monologue: 15 minutes each. No cross talk.

Inquire into the difference between times you have felt a should or should not with any of the precepts and times you have experienced being one with a precept. Consider acting with and without a "Why?" and a "Because . . ."

Discuss together as long as you like.

22

From *Not* to *Non*

Opening to the suchness of stealing and no-stealing.

To stay with the example of stealing and to make use of some of what we have been considering here with Dogen's help, we can begin to see why the precepts are presented as *non* instead of *not* or *don't*. First, if we need *not stealing*—or *don't steal* or *should not steal*—to counter *stealing*, it means that we have *stealing* as a thought or maybe even as a temptation to deal with. Both *stealing* and *not stealing* have become conceptualized, boundaried, and separate from a conceptualized, boundaried *me*. Moreover, in this separation, there is no not stealing without stealing, and in its conceptualized form, there is no stealing without not stealing. They are opposed to, and hence dependent on, each other. Not stealing, when conceptualized, can never be wholehearted. It can never be free of stealing and thus is not liberated. It obstructs and is obstructed by stealing. Stealing becomes something to avoid, to not like, and to resist, and not stealing becomes something to be attached to. This opposition creates a division in us.

There are some morally impeccable people who, even in

the contextual way of understanding the precepts, always do what most of us would consider the right thing to do. They are highly disciplined in following the precepts. Yet not only is there a separation between them and the precept in question but also an inner division, and therefore a price to pay in the lack of freedom and compassion that results. The way of working with the precepts recommended in this book—learning to recognize, allow, and even welcome the stealer in us—helps loosen the hold stealing has on us, or the hold we have on it. That, then, opens us up to the possibility of becoming one with it, which leads to the discovery of its emptiness and thus its boundarylessness, its suchness. It may come as a surprise that, along with a horse's mouth and a donkey's jaw, even stealing, lying, and so on can appear in their suchness. In a section on suchness ("Immo") in his *Shōbōgenzō*, given here in two translations, Dogen addresses this:

> Because trouble too is such a thing, it is not trouble. Also one should not be surprised at such a thing's being such. Even if there is suchness which seems strange, this too is such—there is suchness of "one should not be surprised."[1]

> Because anxiety is itself an essence of thusness, it is not anxiety. Moreover, we need not be startled by the essence of thusness being this way. Even if thusness appears startling and suspicious, it is thusness all the same: there is that thusness by which you ought to be startled.[2]

As we know by now, it isn't just plum blossoms that we can experience in their suchness but also donkeys' jaws and broken wooden ladles. And, of course, in many haiku poems we are presented with the possibility of experiencing lice, fleas, horse piss, itchy dogs, and more in their suchness. Both these translations show us that anxiety, also translated as "trouble," can be experienced in its suchness, its emptiness, its nonconceptuality. And as that, they cease being *what* they are. The same is true of stealing and not stealing. Not stealing is a "good" version of a negative, human, egoic tendency—namely, stealing. It is its opposite. Non-stealing, on the other hand, has no opposite. Like the Tibetan medicines, also known as "wisdoms," mentioned in chapter 20, it is totally self-fulfilling.

As Bodhidharma, the First Zen Patriarch, says of non-stealing, "Self-nature is subtle and mysterious. In the realm of the unattainable Dharma, not arousing the thought of gain is called the Precept of Non-Stealing." In the "ultimate" realm, the thought of gain not arising is not the opposite of anything. There is no thought of gain to resist in order to live the precept of non-stealing. But if in the suchness of not stealing it is no longer not stealing, why, then, do we have non-stealing as a teaching at all? Why aren't we just free of the whole thing, off in some precept-free nirvana land where there is no difference between, say, non-stealing and non-lying? No, we are still here in our complicated life—"the whole hurly-burly,"[3] as Wittgenstein called it. We have non-stealing, not non-lying, because of the context. If they become nonconceptual, don't they lose their identity? Their conceptual identity, yes, but not their unique particularity.

We can recall Dogen's teaching that "'the total experience of a single thing' does not deprive a thing of its own unique particularity. It places a thing neither against others nor against none."[4]

The context would be one in which stealing might occur, not lying or being intoxicated, but we don't know this by conceptually thinking it out. The money that slipped out of the pocket of the person walking ahead of me makes it obvious. This is prajna. Dogen's commentary on non-stealing is: "The self and things of the world are just as they are. The gate of emancipation is open." Both subject and object are "unstained." Both stealing and not stealing are unstained. There is nothing lacking in the realm of self-nature. Therefore, the thought of gain wouldn't even arise. Both stealing and not stealing have been liberated to become non-stealing.

It occurs to me that an experience I occasionally have with homeless people asking for a handout is an example of non-stingy instead of not stingy. I live in New York City, where it is rare not to encounter homelessness anytime one is outdoors. If I am asked for money, I will give something. The fact that there is no thought about its being a good thing to do makes it non-stingy. It's just automatic. But what is striking to me is what it's like to fail to give something when, in a hurry, I rush by a homeless person—"Oh, I can't be bothered, I'm in a hurry." What happens is that I end up stopping dead in my tracks, turning around, and going back to give something. I am aware that there is no thought, no should or shouldn't. It doesn't even have a name. It just is what it is. It's as if in that moment there is an experience of the suchness of both stingy and not stingy, and thus also of myself. It is sudden, out of time, like my student's experience with his Airbnb mentioned in chapter 14.

We are free to interpenetrate. There are no boundaries, no hindrances, no obstructions. When both stingy and not stingy are free to interpenetrate, non-stingy results. All is liberated—no ground, no goal, no "tied to," no opposition, no "Why?"—and it is out of this that non-stingy naturally and spontaneously arises. It is here that we begin to see why faith was so important to Dogen.

23

The Jukai Ceremony

The great precepts of the Buddhas have been upheld and maintained by the Buddha. Buddhas conferred them to buddhas, and ancestors transmitted them to ancestors. Receiving the precepts transcends the borders of past, present, and future.
—DOGEN

Awakening to the Buddha mind is called "truly receiving the Precepts."
—BODHIDHARMA

Jukai is to manifest yourself as the precepts.
—MAEZUMI ROSHI

SO OFTEN Western Zen students think of the Jukai ceremony as being one in which one becomes a Buddhist, as if it were some kind of conversion ceremony. But even if we correctly think of the ceremony as "taking refuge" in the heart of Buddhist teachings, it still doesn't have to mean becoming a Buddhist, as my Roman Catholic nun friend and student, Joan Kigen Kirby, showed me. Even if one does become a Buddhist, it is certainly not meant to be the taking on of an identity, which would then be a concept, thus excluding what is not Buddhist and ending up obstructing all kinds of things and losing freedom and openness.

I find it remarkable that this refuge ceremony should be about precepts. It's not as if a ceremony for receiving precepts is a common occurrence in other traditions. It shows how seriously they are taken in the Zen tradition but, as we have seen, not as mere ethical guidelines for practice. Rather, they are understood to be an aspect of the Absolute, True Nature, or Buddha-nature—they are intrinsic to enlightenment.

The monastic precepts developed in early Buddhism were far greater in number than the Sixteen Bodhisattva Precepts inherited from Dogen. They were intended to set the standards for the conduct of monks. Eventually in the Japanese Soto sect they were reduced to these sixteen and given to lay as well as monastic practitioners. In the eighteenth century there occurred a debate about whether the ceremony of receiving the precepts was simply about making a commitment to follow the teachings of the Buddha, which involved being admitted to a community and living by the precepts, or whether it was about something much more—namely, becoming a buddha, which would entail a completely different relationship to the precepts. The latter view won out in these debates, and looking carefully at the words used in the Jukai ceremony as it has come down to us in the Soto sect, we can see that in a sense it is intended to reveal the buddhahood of the participants and not just confirm their status as new members of a community. In other words, the ceremony is not so much about becoming a Buddhist, as it is about becoming a buddha.

All we have to do to see this is to look at the language of "being one with" spoken by both preceptor and recipient at various points in the ceremony. For example, what Buddhists often call "taking refuge in" the Three Treasures (Buddha, Dharma, Sangha), a language that makes it sound as if they are separate from us, becomes instead "revealing oneself as" the Three Treasures. The preceptor says, "Be one with" each of the Three Treasures, starting with Buddha, and the recipient responds, "Being one with . . . " The preceptor then "transmits" the precepts, which have been "revealed and handed down" through many generations of the lineage. The precepts themselves are "revealed." In other words, they are discovered or uncovered, and not invented or determined by us human beings. In Bernie Glassman's version that my sangha uses, just before giving the precepts the preceptor says, "In order to transmit to you the precepts, I must be in the space of not knowing and manifest as Vairocana Buddha, the Buddha of Formless Forms." In other words, the preceptor becomes the formlessness—Bodhidharma's "wondrous self-nature" out of which the precepts manifest as formless forms, namely, as their suchness. After giving the precepts, the preceptor says, "When sentient beings receive the precepts they enter the realm of the Buddhas." The ceremony ends with those who have already received the precepts greeting the new recipients by circumambulating them, bowing, and saying, "Buddha recognizes Buddha and Buddha bows to Buddha" over and over again. They don't say, "Buddhist bows to Buddhist." Bodhidharma, the First Zen Patriarch, sums this up by saying,

> Receiving is transmission; transmission is awakening. This means that awakening to the Buddha Mind is called "truly receiving the Precepts."

Dogen's version of this is,

> When beings receive the precepts, they attain the level of all Buddhas. They are truly the children of the Buddhas.

24

Being a Buddha

The assertion that after becoming a Buddha, one should discontinue spiritual discipline and engage in no further endeavor is due to an ordinary person's view that does not yet understand the way of buddhas and ancestors.

—DOGEN

AT THE END of the last chapter, we read Dogen's and Bodhidharma's teachings that to receive the precepts means to attain the level of all Buddhas or to awaken to the Buddha Mind. This has nothing to do with some permanent something separate from us way off in the future as a result of many years of practice. As Dogen tells us,

> At the time of the initial desire for enlightenment, one becomes a Buddha, and at the final stage of buddhahood, one [still] becomes a buddha.[1]

> If you have attained enlightenment, you should not halt the practice of the Way by thinking of your present state as final, for the Way is infinite.

> Exert yourself in the Way ever more, even after enlightenment.[2]

The Jukai ceremony itself is an occasion on which we, even as beginners, become a buddha. But how can we *become* a buddha if we already *are* a buddha? One might ask, since we don't *have* Buddha-nature but *are* Buddha-nature, how does it make sense to say that we can *become* a buddha? We may be buddhas, but we don't know it. The ceremony *reveals* to us that we *are* buddhas. Having given the precepts maybe twenty-five or more times, I am always struck by how moving it is to the recipient. It is an example of a momentary experience out of time. But more importantly for Dogen, even though we are buddhas, we have to *actualize* our buddhahood. As Dogen puts it,

> Although this incomparable Dharma is abundant in each person, it is not actualized without practice, and not attained without realization.[3]

This means that the more we practice, the more those moments occur until eventually we start recognizing them for what they are. These moments of becoming a buddha remain moments. They are leaps out of the conceptual.

In addition, he tells us,

> There are some bodhisattvas who became Buddhas countless billions and billions of times.[4]

This helps us see why actualizing a buddha is not to be in some permanent, unchanging, timeless, absolute state, forever free from what Dogen calls our "topsy-turvy everyday life."[5] Moreover, he reminds us that "the vertiginous confusions of life are limitless."[6] Bernie Glassman, in answer to the question, "What is Zen?" always said, "Zen is life." And let's face it, life is infinitely complex and ever changing. As mentioned in chapter 22, Wittgenstein calls it "the whole hurly-burly." In fact, everything that makes up what we call life is impermanent, and as Dogen shows us, that impermanence itself is Buddha-nature. It is a boundless dynamism in which nothing is excluded. "All existence is Buddha-nature" (*Bussho*, tr., Kim),[7] even what he calls our "vast and giddy karmic consciousness."[8] The question is, can we know all the conceptualized aspects of life in their suchness, just as they are without preferences or stories? Can we know them by being them, instead of watching life flow by as if we were standing on the banks of the river life?

"Becoming" is the revealing of what we already are. It's a discovery, not a process, but what we already are needs to be *actualized* over and over again until we begin to "live out of" it. Buddha-nature itself is impermanent. It is not sitting somewhere waiting for us, nor is it a seed in us, a potential plant. We can see this expressed by the fact that even though receiving the precepts is to become a buddha, the Jukai ceremony ends by, nevertheless, asking the recipient after she has received each precept, "Will you maintain it?" The phrase "not actualized without practice" makes it sound as if practice were the means to actualization, but it is rather that practice itself *is* the actualizing of this incomparable Dharma. And practice isn't some once-and-for-all condition or state. After all, some bodhisattvas became buddhas "countless billions and billions of times." There is one Christian mystic I know of who sounds like Dogen in this regard, and that is Mechthild von Magdeburg:

> Therefore renounce all fear and shame and all outer virtues. The virtue alone which you carry inside by nature, this you will want to find over and over, for eternity.[9]

I think I would precede "renounce" with "by compassionately allowing, welcoming, and becoming one with" all fear and shame of the killer, liar, stealer, and so forth. Many years ago, when I first began practice with Bernie, I had the experience of "the scales falling from my eyes." It was during a *mondo*, the public exchange between student and teacher, when a man who, like me, was a philosophy professor, but also a very politically active person, came up, did his bows, and then asked his question in the form of a political complaint about Zen. Bernie answered by simply saying, "There are no utopias. It's like cleaning—the job is never done once and for all." Hearing this profoundly affected me, and all these years later, I appreciate how much of Dogen was in Bernie's teaching.

Dogen is, as we know, famous for saying that practice is enlightenment and not a means to the supposed end of enlightenment. But what exactly is practice? We usually think of "practice" as particular formal Zen practices, especially zazen, but think about the word *practice*. It implies action, activity, conduct, and so forth—all the "doings" of life: walking slowly, walking fast, changing diapers, eating oatmeal, doing a retreat at Auschwitz, seeing a butterfly, making love, hearing a crow, holding the hand of someone who is dying, canvassing for a candidate, peeing, shitting, drinking tea, speaking, and even thinking. As Dogen's term *total exertion* makes clear, this is not a question of "mindfulness" practice. Mindfulness is very important, but we don't eat oatmeal with our minds. We need a hand, a spoon, an arm to lift the spoon, lips, teeth, a tongue, swallowing, and more. We are also a whole body sitting somehow somewhere. Even seeing, hearing, feeling cold or hot are "doings." The important thing for Zen is to be "one with" those doings—namely, doing whatever it is 100 percent, which doesn't happen once and for all.

Total exertion applies to both sides of the oneness relation. When we do something 100 percent, there is no room left for self-consciousness, hence for a self—that is, for something I could describe by making myself an object. As in the story about the cold presented in chapter 12, we are "killed," but so are the concepts we put on the particulars of reality. In totally exerting ourselves in openness, we allow those particulars to exert themselves. The two of us become one, the oneness of suchness. This is the nonduality of duality, the move from *not* to *non*, the opening to oneness with the Zen precepts.

APPENDIX 1

Bodhidharma and Dogen's Commentaries on the Zen Precepts

Bodhidharma's commentary

1. Non-killing
Self-nature is subtle and mysterious. In the realm of the everlasting Dharma, not giving rise to the idea of killing is called the Precept of Non-killing.

2. Non-stealing
Self-nature is subtle and mysterious. In the realm of the unattainable dharma, not arousing the thought of gain is called the Precept of Non-stealing.

3. Non-misusing of Sex
Self-nature is subtle and mysterious. In the realm of the ungilded Dharma, not creating a veneer of attachment is called the Precept of Non-misusing Sex.

4. Non-lying
Self-nature is subtle and mysterious. In the realm of the inexplicable Dharma, not preaching a single word is called the Precept of Non-lying.

5. Non-giving or Taking Drugs
Self-nature is subtle and mysterious. In the realm of the intrinsically pure Dharma, not giving rise to delusions is called the Precept of Non-giving or Taking Drugs.

6. Non-discussing Faults of Others
Self-nature is subtle and mysterious. In the realm of the flawless Dharma, not expounding upon error is called the Precept of Non-speaking of Faults of Others.

7. Non-blaming Others and Elevating Oneself
Self-nature is subtle and mysterious. In the realm of the equitable Dharma, not dwelling upon I against you is called the Precept of Non-praising Yourself while Abusing Others.

8. Non-being Stingy
Self-nature is subtle and mysterious. In the genuine, all-pervading Dharma, not being stingy about a single thing is called the Precept of Non-sparing the Dharma Assets.

9. Non-anger
Self-nature is subtle and mysterious. In the realm of the selfless Dharma, not contriving reality for the self is called the Precept of No-Indulging in Anger.

10. Non-defaming the Three Treasures
Self-nature is subtle and mysterious. In the realm of the One, not holding nihilistic concepts of ordinary beings and sages is called the Precept of Not Defaming the Three Treasures.

Dogen's commentary

1. Non-killing
The Buddha seed grows in accordance with not taking life. Transmit the life of Buddha's wisdom and do not kill.

2. Non-stealing
The self and things of the world are just as they are. The gate of emancipation is open.

3. Non-misusing of Sex
The Three Wheels are pure and clear. When you have nothing to desire, you follow the way of all Buddhas.

4. Non-lying
The Dharma Wheel turns from the beginning. There is neither surplus nor lack. The whole universe is moistened with nectar, and the truth is ready to harvest.

5. Non-giving or Taking Drugs
Drugs are not brought in yet. Don't let them invade. That is the great light.

6. Non-discussing the Faults of Others
In the Buddha Dharma, there is one path, one Dharma, one realization, one practice. Don't permit fault-finding. Don't permit haphazard talk.

7. Non-blaming Others and Elevating Oneself
Buddhas and Ancestral Teachers realize the empty sky and

the great earth. When they manifest the noble body, there is neither inside nor outside in emptiness. When they manifest the Dharma body, there is not even a bit of earth on the ground.

8. Non-stinginess

One phrase, one verse—that is the ten thousand things and one hundred grasses; one dharma, one realization—that is all Buddhas and Ancestral Teachers. Therefore, from the beginning, there has been no stinginess at all.

9. Non-anger

Not advancing, not retreating, not real, not empty. There is an ocean of bright clouds. There is an ocean of solemn clouds.

10. Non-abusing the Three Treasures

The teisho of the actual body is the harbor and the weir. This is the most important thing in the world. Its virtue finds its home in the ocean of essential nature. It is beyond explanation. We just accept it with respect and gratitude.

APPENDIX 2

The Three Pure Precepts and Bodhidharma

BY BERNIE GLASSMAN

WHEN I WAS first taught the meaning of the word *kai*, my teacher used the translation "aspects of life" instead of "precepts," and I prefer to think of kai as the aspects of our life. I would like to talk about this in the context of the Three Pure Precepts and a koan. The Three Pure Precepts are cease from evil, do good, and do good for others. The koan is a simple one, the fourth case of *The Gateless Gate*. The main case, the koan itself, is one question: "Why does the Western barbarian have no beard?" As you probably know, it refers to Bodhidharma, who came from the West (India) to China. As you probably also know, one of the metaphors or expressions in our tradition that's very common is the question, "Why did Bodhidharma come to the East?" It's a metaphor for the question "What is Zen?" We say that Zen is kai, is life. So, what is this Zen? What is life we are talking about? If Zen is kai, if it's life itself, then what's the point of talking about bringing it from one country to another? What are you transmitting? What is the Dharma torch that can't—shouldn't—be extinguished? These are the questions in that koan.

Of course, Bodhidharma is not some figure that lived many, many years ago. Bodhidharma is us, all of us. It's our teachers that come from Japan, from the West, carrying the torch. It's all of us coming from wherever we came from, gathered here. Why did we come here? What are we carrying? What are our teachers carrying? What is it that we want to receive? And what is it that we don't want to receive?

There are a number of ways of looking at koans. One is that we use them to illustrate points. We talk about them. I'm using one now to illustrate something, and I'm talking about it. Another, which has to do with actual koan practice, is to become the koan. In this case, become the Western barbarian! Become the beard! Become Bodhidharma! To pass the koan is to experience the state that's being presented, being Bodhidharma.

This first condition of being brings us to the first pure precept: ceasing from evil. Dogen Zenji in his instructions on kai says about the first pure precept, "Ceasing from evil, this is the abiding place of laws and rules of all Buddhas." "This abiding place," this source, this is the state the koan wants us to experience, the state of nonduality, the state of not knowing, the state of non-separation. The sixth ancestor in China, Hui-neng, defines zazen as the state of mind in which there is no separation between subject and object, no space between I and thou, you and me, up and down, right or wrong. This ceasing from evil, the abiding place, is the state of at-one-ment, of being one, of being Buddha, of being the Three Treasures, of Be-ing, of returning to the

One. That's a very difficult place to be in. This is the place where we don't know what's right, what's wrong. This is the place of just being, of life itself, of kai itself. How many of us can say that we are open to all the ways of all lives, of all beings and non-beings and spirits? How many of us can say that we don't have the answer, the right way? Or how many of us can say that every way that's being presented is the right way?

Zen is a practice that pushes us to experience, to realize, to actualize what is. We human beings possess a number of characteristics that separate us from that experience. One is the brain. The brain thinks dualistically. That's the way it functions. Concerning some parts of ourselves—for example, our stomachs—we don't think dualistically. I don't go around being aware of having a stomach unless, of course, something is wrong with it. If I have a pain, there is a sense of separation. If you experience the oneness of life, you would not ask the question "Is that the other or not?" If you experience the oneness of life, you would just function naturally.

Recently a term that has come up for me and seems to have a lot of meaning in my life is *bearing witness*. For me, zazen becomes a form of bearing witness to the Three Treasures, bearing witness to life, bearing witness to the elimination of the denial of the oneness of our life. As human beings, each one of us is denying something. Each one of us is aware of certain aspects of life that we do not want to deal with, usually because we are afraid of them. Sometimes it's society that is in denial about certain of its aspects, and we go along with it. Zazen in its true state allows us to bear witness to all life, and for me, that's the second pure precept: doing good. Dogen Zenji says, "Doing good, this is the Dharma, of *samyak-sambodhi.* This is the way of all beings."

A symptom of separation, a symptom of duality, is found in the word *why*. Many koans start with that. "Why has Bodhidharma, the Western barbarian, no beard?" Why! That's the symptom of duality. Why do we put on the robe at the sound of the bell? Why do we do this, do that? Why do we need rules and regulations? Why do we need forms? Why this form? Why is grass green? Couldn't it be purple? I like purple. Grass is green, therefore I don't like it. So why? Eliminate the word *why* and again we come back to bearing witness. Recently I thought of Shakyamuni's life, and I thought of his father trying to isolate him from suffering, from old age and death, from renunciates. And for me that became a metaphor for the denial of, or separation from, those aspects of ourselves or of society that we are afraid of or not ready to deal with. These are all those things that lead to the aspects of myself that I've been in denial about and am afraid of and those aspects of society that I'm afraid of or deny.

For me, the importance of bearing witness to what is denied grew out of my zazen, out of the bearing witness to life as a whole and what arose out of that. When I bear witness, I learn, I open to what is. There's a healing process in that. The root of the word *ceremonies* is this "healing," and for me, one of the most important ceremonies is this bearing witness. This is all the second pure precept. Bearing witness to things that I am denying or that society is denying. Bearing witness to the things I don't want to deal with. So, in terms of our koan, being Bodhidharma, just feeling the beard, being the beard, we see all the problems—the food that gets stuck in the beard, the molds that grow. We learn how to clean it, how to comb it, how to become one with it, how to be Bodhidharma. Taking care. It's a tremendous healing and learning. The beard teaches us. And the things that we are in denial about teach us. We don't go to them to teach them. They teach us. And they teach when we can listen, can bear witness. And to bear witness is, again, to me zazen, being one with those things.

A student of mine is walking, along with seventy other people, from Auschwitz in Poland to Hiroshima, a five-thousand-mile walk through many war-torn countries. He told me that one of the things that was happening on the walk is that many of the people with him are walking but not experiencing the suffering going on in those countries. They are doing it but staying out if it. They see soldiers and they are afraid to talk to them. They see prisoners and they're afraid to talk to them. He called it "spiritual correctness"—doing the right thing but not allowing oneself to become it. That's a danger of our practice. We can learn all the right things. We can talk about all the right things but not allow ourselves to be them.

For me, the flowering of zazen, the flowering of bearing witness, is the third pure precept: doing good for others. Dogen Zenji says, "This is to transcend the profane and to be beyond the holy. This is to liberate oneself and others." Many years ago in Los Angeles, I had an experience in which I felt—I saw—the suffering of the hungry spirits. I was surrounded by all kinds of suffering beings. Almost immediately I made a vow to serve them, to feed them. How do we feed them? "Raising the Bodhi Mind, the supreme meal is offered" are words in our liturgy. That's the food for the hungry spirits. Raising the Bodhi Mind, the supreme meal is offered. So, there are two parts of our practice: raising the Bodhi Mind, ascending the mountain, is one; and the other is offering, descending the mountain. What good is it if we just make ourselves more holy? What's the point? The point is to serve, to offer, to be the offering. Of itself the fruit is born. So out of our zazen, out of our bearing witness, we don't have to worry about what we ought to do. If we cease from evil, if we become that state of unknowing, we become zazen, and the offering will arise. Fruit will be born. In fact, that's what each of us is. We can appreciate all the fruit in this wonderful garden that some call "the universe." There was a priest from Korea who started working with the children who were retarded orphans. And through the monastery he ordained the children. What was beautiful to me of what he said was that the children he worked with were Buddhas. He ordained them so he could take care of the Buddhas, not so he could make the children into something that we would accept. He accepted each child as he or she was—as the Buddha—and served and took care. It could also be said that in the eyes of the Buddha we are all retarded. In my case, because of my karma, my life has evolved into working or trying to work with society as a whole, as a Dharma field. And I really feel it is directly out of that experience I had. And this leads me into what I do.

As I mentioned earlier, the first pure precept, ceasing from evil, we can call "returning to the One." And you know there is another famous koan, "Where does the One return to?" We answered it in the beginning and throughout this talk: The One returns to life. Zen is life. And if so, what can be excluded? Always questions come up: How do we bring our Zen into our life? But Zen is life. What's there to bring? Into what? So the point is to see life as the practice field. Every aspect of our life has to become practice. What is practice? In the work I do, I take that circle of life and I look at it in terms of the five Buddha families. That's just a scheme. My background is mathematics, and I love schemes. You can have many different schemes for how to break up the circle of life. But for me, I use the five Buddha families, our mandala. We call it the "Greyston Mandala." In the center of the mandala, the center of the circle, is the Buddha family, the formless forms, the state of nonduality, the first pure precept, non-knowing. It's the foundation of the network of the work we do that is represented by the other four families.

When we went to New York, we first established the Buddha family, the practice of zazen, the practice of meditation retreats, the establishment of an atmosphere of no duality. The next family that we looked at was Ratna, "right livelihood." The next was the Karma family, which I called "social action." Karma, as you know, is action, right action. The next was Vajra, which I call "study"; not study abstractly but study of life as it is, as we are doing it. And the fifth, Padma, I call "relationship" or "integration." It's the energy that keeps it all whole. As dualistically thinking human beings, we think whatever we happen to be doing is the right thing. Nothing else is good. It's the same as we look at society. We create livelihoods and social action and we think, "Oh, this is essence, not that." How to keep all this integrated as one circle of life—that's the Padma energy.

Being trained in a practice that comes out of a monastic model whose forms make the environment conducive to our getting to this state of not knowing, to seeing the oneness of life, the question for me is what are the forms in business or social action that are conducive to seeing the oneness in society, in life? What are the forms that exist now? What keeps us from bearing witness? What keeps us from seeing oneness, life, from appreciating everything as it is? What is it that makes us move toward that conditioning of thinking that we know the right way? So, my life at this point is dedicated to trying to create an environment, a form, not just for us as individuals but for society, that deals with this issue. How do we create the forms that will be conducive to moving each of us toward the realization, the actualization, of the enlightened way?

Just doing zazen doesn't necessarily lead into a position of nonduality. So, what else can we do? It's the role of the teacher to try to answer this.

What are the *upaya*, the methods, the expedient means? What are the forms that can help us get into that situation where's it's easier for us to experience that state of nonduality? Almost anything we do will cause more dualistic thinking. So how do we lead ourselves, our brothers, our sisters into a state of nonduality? That's the question. That's koan. I can give you as a concrete example a form that we created in business that I think helps people. Originally our businesses were places for training our residents, and that is still in some cases true. Then we opened our business to folks who were homeless and unemployed and very poor. The majority of our staff were folks who were either homeless or chronically unemployed or people that had tremendously high-paying jobs selling dope, crack. Some of these latter made a fortune and then on their own decided to change their lifestyle. We've hired many people like that. A lot of them come in with the notion that what they need are things for themselves. To help them get a glimpse of the interdependence of life, we created teams of people working. How they get paid is a function of how their team produces. So if someone on the team doesn't know the job very well, it behooves the rest to teach that person, because then they all make more money. So, we've created a form to bring their consciousness just a little bit away from thinking how they are going to improve for themselves. It's still how they are going to make money, but now it's in terms of the whole group. Moving people into the framework of seeing the interdependence of life then allows the next step to unfold, the next, and the next. So those are forms we've developed in addition to the practice of non-separation, of zazen. But that's the koan: How do you do things like that? How do you do things in the monastery to make sure that you don't become attached to your way of doing it as the only way, the best way, so that everyone else out there who's not doing it your way doesn't know what's "doing"? How do you do that? Those are, for me, the interesting questions.

To take another example, you know that *sesshin*, the Zen word for retreat, means to unify mind. I work with people who are homeless. For me that means that I need to try to unify the mind with those living in the streets. To do this, I started giving street retreats. It isn't necessary, but I needed to do it. I have to make it clear that my doing street retreats was not doing a homeless retreat. Many people call these "homeless retreats," but to unify the mind with somebody homeless, you have to be homeless. Everyone I took with me, including myself, knew that we were going back to our homes in a week. We were street people but not homeless people. The ceremony of ordaining, *shuke tokudo*, means "leaving home." So in some sense, if one can really do shuke tokudo, you can do street retreats. But that's a separate story. So a street retreat is being at one with those living in the street. How do you know that? You live in the street. So that's what I did with everyone who came. We lived in the street. Now part of life is breathing, part of life is eating, part of life is doing zazen. I don't look at them as special. They are just what I do each day . . . I don't breathe to live. Because I'm alive I breathe. I don't do zazen to become something. Because I'm alive I do zazen. So, a street retreat has all those elements. It has eating, sleeping, going to the bathroom. It has all the aspects of your life except you happen to be living in the street. So the rules change. There are no bathrooms, no showers, no zafus, zabutons. You sit on the floor. We had no beautiful drums or robes, so we used garbage cans or whatever we could find for liturgy. But every day we had service. Every day we sat. But it was difficult, even just to get people together again after they had been separated to find food or bathrooms. I was amazed at what happened on that first street retreat. There were people who joined me—for example, my senior disciple, my first dharma successor, Peter Matthiessen, who has done many things in his life and has probably done hundreds of sesshins. There are all kinds of people, some came for one day and some for five days, but every one of them told me it was the most powerful experience of their life. Something happened. I think it's the immediacy. Sesshin also brings us to the immediacy of life. But the street does it very, very dramatically. Issues of eating, peeing, defecating, every aspect of our life is raw and right there. And denial. One day on the street and people deny you. When you walk into a restaurant, they won't serve you, won't let you in. When you have to go to the bathroom desperately, you go into a restaurant and ask if you can use the bathroom, and they say no. People walk away from you because they don't like the way you smell or look. If you truly experience this, you will never avoid those people again, those people that were you. That's the power of the street and what it can teach, the immediacy of now. It teaches us to bear witness.

So if you can just feel "his beard" and see all its problems —the food that gets stuck in it, the molds that grow in it, its tangles—if you can see how to clean it, comb it, and then become one with it, that's a tremendous healing and learning. The beard teaches, and the things you are in denial about will teach you. They will teach you if you can listen, bear witness, and then become at-one with them. This is zazen. This is the Three Pure Precepts.

Notes

Introduction

1. Hee-Jin Kim, *Eihei Dōgen: Mystical Realist* (Somerville, MA: Wisdom Publications, 2004).
2. From Dogen's *Shōbōgenzō*,"Bukkyō" (On What the Buddha Taught), *in Shōbōgenzō: The Treasure House of the Eye of the True Teaching—a Trainee's Translation of Great Master Dogen's Spiritual Masterpiece*, trans. Hubert Nearman (Mount Shasta, CA: Shasta Abbey Press, 2007), 307.
3. John Daido Loori, *Invoking Reality: Moral and Ethical Teachings of Zen* (Mt. Tremper, NY: Dharma Communications, 1998). This book was reissued by Tuttle as *The Heart of Being: Moral and Ethical Teachings of Zen Buddhism*, and Daido Roshi's translation and analysis of Dogen's "Kyōjukaimon" is in chapter 2. He also wrote on the topic of Zen ethics and the precepts in *Invoking Reality: Moral and Ethical Teachings of Zen* (Boulder, CO: Shambhala Publications, 2007).
4. Keizan Jokin, *The Record of Transmitting the Light: Zen Master Keizan's* Denkoroku, trans. Francis Dojun Cook (Somerville, MA: Wisdom Publications, 2021), 47.
5. From Dogen's *Shōbōgenzō*, "Genjō Kōan" (Actualizing the Fundamental Point), trans. Robert Aitken and Kazuaki Tanahashi, in *Moon in a Dewdrop: Writings of Zen Master Dogen*, ed. Kazuaki Tanahashi (New York: North Point Press, 1985), 70.
6. From Dogen's *Shōbōgenzō*, "Zuimonki" (Record of Things Heard), trans. Shohaku Okumura (Japan: Shotoshu Shumucho, 2018), 24.
7. Some teachers use the term *literal* for this level, but it doesn't seem to bring out its "never ever" aspect.

8. Confucius, *Analects*, trans. James Legge (Los Angeles: USC US-China Institute, 1901), chap. 2.
9. Augustine of Hippo, *Homilies on the First Epistle of John* (Hyde Park, NY: New City Press, 2008).
10. Angelus Silesius, *The Cherubic Wanderer (Classics of Western Spirituality)*, trans. Meria Shrady (New York: Paulist Press, 1986), 53.
11. Meister Eckhart, *Meister Eckhart: Teacher and Preacher*, ed. Bernard McGinn, trans. Frank Tobin (Mahwah, NJ: Paulist Press, 1986), 278.
12. From Dogen's *Shōbōgenzō*,"Shinjin Gakudō" (Learning through the Body and the Mind), in *Shōbōgenzō: The Eye and Treasury of the True Law*, trans. Kōsen Nishiyama and John Stevens (Tokyo: Nakayam Shobō Japan Publications, 1988), 33; available at https://terebess.hu/zen/dogen/nishiyama.pdf, accessed Jan. 6, 2022.
13. Hakuin Ekaku, "The Four Cognitions," in *Kensho: The Heart of Zen*, trans. and ed. Thomas Cleary (Boston: Shambhala Publications, 1997), 77–82. Bracketed text added by author.
14. From Dogen's *Shōbōgenzō*, "Sanjūshichihon Bodaibumpō" (Thirty-Seven Qualities of Enlightenment), in *Dōgen on Meditation and Thinking: A Reflection on His View of Zen*, trans. Hee-Jin Kim (Albany: State University of New York Press, 2007), 86.

Part One Introduction: Working with the Precepts by Acknowledging the Killer in Us

1. Keizan Jokin, *The Record of Transmitting the Light: Zen Master Keizan's* Denkoroku, trans. Francis Dojun Cook (Somerville, MA: Wisdom Publications, 2021), 47.
2. From Dogen's *Shōbōgenzō*,"Sanjūshichihon Bodaibumpō" (Thirty-Seven Qualities of Enlightenment), in *Dōgen on Meditation and Thinking: A Reflection of His View of Zen*, trans. Hee-Jin Kim (Albany: State University of New York Press, 2007), 138n10.
3. See "The Three Tenets," Zen Peacemakers, accessed November 3, 2021, https://zenpeacemakers.org/the-three-tenets/.
4. Kasyapa was the first successor to the Buddha, the one who smiled when the Buddha twirled a flower, and who got the deep, hidden Zen meaning behind the twirling and in the Buddha's speaking.
5. Keizan Jokin, *Record of Transmitting the Light*, 245.

Chapter 1. Non-killing

1. Muriel Rukeyser, "St. Roach," in *A Muriel Rukeyser Reader* (New York: W. W. Norton, 1994), 255.
2. Stephen Batchelor, *Verses from the Center: A Buddhist Version of the Sublime* (New York: Riverhead Press, 2001), 19.

Chapter 2. Non-stealing

1. Ch'i-chi, "White Hair," trans. Burton Watson, in *The Clouds Should Know Me by Now: Buddhist Monks of China*, ed. Red Pine and Mike O'Connor (Somerville, MA: Wisdom Publications, 1998).
2. Keizan Jokin, *The Record of Transmitting the Light: Zen Master Keizan's Denkoroku*, trans. Francis Dojun Cook (Somerville, MA: Wisdom Publications, 2021), 161.

Chapter 3. Non-misusing Sex

1. Robert Aitken, *The Mind of Clover: Essays in Zen Buddhist Ethics* (San Francisco: North Point Press, 1984), 38.
2. Wendell Berry, *The Unsettling of America: Culture and Agriculture* (Berkeley, CA: Counterpoint Press, 2015).
3. John Daido Loori, *Invoking Reality: Moral and Ethical Teachings of Zen* (Mt. Tremper, NY: Dharma Communications, 1998), 83.

Chapter 4. Non-lying

1. Sōiku Shigematsu, trans., *A Zen Forest: Sayings of the Masters* (New York: Weatherhill, 1981), no. 156.
2. Shigematsu, *Zen Forest*, no. 12.
3. Koun Yamada, trans., *The Gateless Gate* (Boston: Wisdom Publications, 2004), case no. 36, 177.
4. Yamada, *Gateless Gate*, case no. 43, 204.
5. Dogen, *The Zen Poetry of Dogen*, trans. and ed. Steven Heine (Boston: Tuttle Publishing, 1997), 103.
6. From Dogen's *Shōbōgenzō*, "Mujō Seppō" (Insentient Beings Speak Dharma), in Masanobu Takahashi, *Essence of Dogen*, trans. Yuzuru Nobuoka (London: Kegan Paul, 1983), 17.

Chapter 5. Non-misusing Intoxicants

1. Rumi, *The Essential Rumi*, trans. Coleman Barks (San Francisco: HarperCollins, 1995), 5–6.
2. Thomas Merton, *The Inner Experience: Notes on Contemplation* (New York: Harper Collins, 2004), 126.
3. Zen Master Bassui, *Mud and Water: The Collected Teachings of Zen Master Bassui*, trans. Arthur Braverman (Boston: Wisdom Publications, 2002), 13.
4. Kodo Sawaki Roshi, "The Dharma Words of Homeless Kodo," in *Shikantaza: An Introduction to Zazen*, recorded by Uchiyama Kosho Roshi, trans. Shohaku Okumura (Japan: Kyoto Soto-Zen Center, 1985), 119.
5. Dogen, "Death Poem," trans. Philip Whalen and Kazuaki Tanahashi, in *Moon in a Dewdrop: Writings of Zen Master Dogen*, ed. Kazuaki Tanahashi (New York: North Point Press, 1985), 219.

Chapter 6. Non-talking About Others' Errors and Faults

1. John Daido Loori, *Invoking Reality: Moral and Ethical Teachings of Zen* (Mt. Tremper, NY: Dharma Communications, 1998), 93. Italics added.

Chapter 7. Non-elevating Oneself and Blaming Others

1. Herbert Fingarette, *The Self in Transformation* (New York: HarperCollins, 1965).
2. Muriel Rukeyser, "Despisals," in *A Muriel Ruckeyser Reader* (New York: W. W. Norton, 1994), 246.
3. Thich Nhat Hanh, "Please Call Me by My True Names," in *Call Me by My True Names: The Collected Poems of Thich Nhat Hanh* (Berkeley, CA: Parallax Press, 1999), 72–73.

Chapter 8. Non-being Stingy

1. Rumi, "Dervish at the Door," *The Essential Rumi*, trans. Coleman Barks (San Francisco: HarperCollins, 1995), 116.
2. For an extraordinary version of what a grace before meals could be, see Mary Oliver's poem "Rice" in *New and Selected Poems, Volume One* (Boston: Beacon Press, 1992), 38.

3. Mary Oliver, "Have You Ever Tried to Enter the Long Black Branches," in *West Wind: Poems and Prose Poems* (Boston: Houghton Mifflin, 1997), 61.
4. Keizan Jokin, *The Record of Transmitting the Light: Zen Master Keizan's* Denkoroku, trans. Francis Dojun Cook (Somerville, MA: Wisdom Publications, 2021), 189.
5. Keizan, *Denkoroku*, 42.
6. Keizan, *Denkoroku*, 69.
7. Dogen, *The Zen Poetry of Dogen*, trans. Steven Heine (Boston: Tuttle Publishing, 1997), 93.
8. Mary Oliver, "The Kookaburras," in *New and Selected Poems, Volume One* (Boston: Beacon Press, 1992), 87.

Chapter 9. Non-being Angry

1. Aristotle, *Nicomachean Ethics*, trans. J. A. K. Thomson (London: Penguin Books, 1955), 101.
2. From a talk Thich Nhat Hanh gave at a Buddhist Peace Fellowship retreat in 1983. Quoted in Robert Aitken, *The Mind of Clover: Essays in Zen Buddhist Ethics* (San Francisco: North Point Press, 1984), 95.

Chapter 10. Non-abusing the Three Treasures

1. Martin Buber, *I and Thou*, trans. Walter Kaufmann (New York: Simon and Schuster, 1970), 123.
2. From Dogen's *Shōbōgenzō*, "Gyobutsu-iigi" (The Dignified Behavior of Acting Buddha), in *Eihei Dōgen: Mystical Realist*, trans. Hee-Jin Kim (Somerville, MA: Wisdom Publications, 2004), 72.
3. Koun Yamada, trans., *The Gateless Gate* (Boston: Wisdom Publications, 2004), case no. 30, 148.
4. Buber, *I and Thou*, trans. Walter Kaufmann, 59 and 55. Italics mine.
5. Joshu, *The Recorded Sayings of Zen Master Joshu*, trans. James Green (Boulder, CO: Shambhala, 2001), 122.
6. Urs App, *Zen Master Yunmen* (Boulder, CO: Shambhala Publications, 2018), 195.

Chapter 11. Different Kinds of Oneness

1. John Blofed, trans., *The Zen Teaching of Huang Po* (Boston: Shambhala, 1994), 47–51.
2. Blofeld, *Zen Teaching of Huang Po*, 69.

3. From Dōgen's *Shōbōgenzō*, "Shoaku-makusa" (Not to Commit Any Evil), in *Eihei Dōgen: Mystical Realist*, trans. Hee-Jin Kim (Boston: Wisdom Publications, 2004), 225.
4. From Dogen's *Shōbōgenzō*, "Bukkyō" (On What the Buddha Taught), in *Shōbōgenzō: The Treasure House of the Eye of the True Teaching—a Trainee's Translation of Great Master Dogen's Spiritual Masterpiece*, trans. Hubert Nearman (Mount Shasta, CA: Shasta Abbey Press, 2007), 301–3.
5. From Dogen's *Shōbōgenzō*, "Sesshin-sesshō" (On Expressing One's True Nature by Expressing One's Intent), in *Shōbōgenzō: The Treasure House of the Eye of the True Teaching*, trans. Hubert Nearman, 535.
6. From Dogen's *Shōbōgenzō*, "Menju" (Face-to-Face Transmission), in *Master Dogen's Shobogenzo, Book* 3, trans. Gudo Nishijima and Chodo Cross (Dogen Sangha, 2006), 134.
7. From Dogen's *Shōbōgenzō*, "Menju," trans. Reb Anderson and Kazuaki Tanahashi, in *Moon in a Dewdrop: Writings of Zen Master Dōgen*, ed. Kazuaki Tanahashi (New York: North Point Press, 1985), 180.
8. From Dogen's *Shōbōgenzō*,"Kaiin-zammai" (Ocean-Reflection Samadhi), in *Flowers of Emptiness: Selections from Dogen's Shobogenzo*, trans. Hee-Jin Kim (Lewiston/Queenston: Edwin Mellen Press, 1985), 167.
9. From Dogen's *Shōbōgenzō*,"Gabyo" (The Pictured Cakes), in *Eihei Dogen*, 66.

Chapter 12. Suchness, Uniqueness, and the Nonconceptual

1. From Dogen's *Shōbōgenzō*, "Kaiin-zammai" (Ocean-Reflection Samadhi), in *Master Dogen's Shobogenzo, Book* 2, trans. Gudo Nishijima and Chodo Cross (Dogen Sangha, 1996), 159.
2. From Dogen's *Shōbōgenzō*, "Gabyo" (The Pictured Cakes), in *Eihei Dogen: Mystical Realist*, trans. Hee-Jin Kim (Boston: Wisdom Publications, 2004), 66.
3. From Dogen's *Shōbōgenzō*, "Sansui-kyō" (Mountains and Waters Sutra), trans. Arnold Kotler and Kazuaki Tanahashi, in *Moon in a Dewdrop: Writings of Zen Master Dogen*, ed. Kazuaki Tanahashi (New York: North Point Press, 1985), 102.
4. From Dogen's *Shōbōgenzō*, "Kai-in-zanmai" (Samadhi, State Like the Sea), in *Master Dogen's Shobogenzo, Book* 2, 161.

5. From Dogen's *Shōbōgenzō*, "Genjo-Koan," (The Realized Universe), in *Master Dogen's Shobogenzo, Book* 2, 28.
6. Dogen, "Dongshan's 'Cold and Heat,'" case no. 225, in *The True Dharma Eye: Zen Master Dōgen's Three Hundred Kōans*, trans. Kazuaki Tanahashi and John Daido Loori (Boulder, CO: Shambhala Publications, 2005), 307.
7. Richard B. Clarke, trans., *Hsin-hsin Ming: Verses on the Faith-Mind by Seng-ts'an, Third Zen Patriarch* (Buffalo, NY: White Pine Press, 1973).
8. Dōgen, *The Wholehearted Way: A Translation of Eihei Dōgen's* Bendowa, *with Commentary by Kōshō Uchiyama Roshi*, trans. Shohaku Okumura and Taigen Daniel Leighton (North Clarendon, VT: Tuttle Publishing, 1997), 19.

Chapter 13. A Defense of Concepts and Language

1. From Dogen's *Shōbōgenzō*, "Mujō Seppō" (Insentient Beings Speak Dharma), in Masanobu Takahashi, *Essence of Dogen*, trans. Yuzuru Nobuoka (London: Kegan Paul, 1983), 17.
2. From Dogen's *Shōbōgenzō*, "Sansui-kyō" (Mountains and Waters Sutra), in *Dōgen on Meditation and Thinking: A Reflection on His View of Zen*, trans. Hee-Jin Kim (Albany: State University of New York Press, 2007), 62.

Chapter 14. Experiencing Suchness

1. Excerpted from Dogen, "The Point of Zazen, after Zen Master Hongzhi," trans. Philip Whalen and Kazuaki Tanahashi, in *Moon in a Dewdrop: Writings of Zen Master Dōgen*, ed. Kazuaki Tanahashi (New York: North Point Press, 1985), 219.
2. Quoted in Bernie Glassman, *Infinite Circle: Teachings in Zen* (Boston: Shambhala Publications, 2003), 77.
3. From Dogen's *Shōbōgenzō*,"Genjō Kōan" (Actualizing the Fundamental Point), trans. Robert Aitken and Kazuaki Tanahashi, in *Moon in a Dewdrop*, 69.
4. From Dogen's *Shōbōgenzō* fascicle "Shinjin Gakudō" (Learning through the Body and the Mind), in *Shōbōgenzō: The Eye and Treasury of the True Law*, trans. Kōsen Nishiyama and John Stevens (Tokyo: Nakayam Shobō Japan Publications, 1988), 33; available at https://terebess.hu/zen/dogen/nishiyama.pdf, accessed January 6, 2022.

5. "Shinjin Gakudō," 33.
6. Martin Buber, *I and Thou*, trans. Walter Kaufmann (New York: Simon and Schuster, 1970), 62.
7. From Dogen's *Shōbōgenzō*,"Yuibutsu Yobutsu" (Only Buddha and Buddha), trans. Ed Brown and Kazuaki Tanahashi, in *Moon in a Dewdrop*,162.
8. From Dogen's *Shōbōgenzō*, "Shōji" (Birth and Death), in *The Heart of Dōgen's Shōbōgenzō*, trans. Norman Waddell and Masao Abe (Albany: State University of New York Press, 2002), 106–7.
9. These words appear throughout Kim's three books on Dogen.

Chapter 15. The Suchness of the Subject

1. From Dogen's *Shōbōgenzō*, "Kaiin-zammai" (Ocean-Reflection Samadhi), in *Flowers of Emptiness: Selections from Dogen's Shobogenzo*, trans. Hee-Jin Kim (Lewiston/Queenston: Edwin Mellen Press, 1985), 167.

Chapter 16. The Samadhi of Self-Fulfilling Activity

1. From Dogen's *Shōbōgenzō*, "Kaiin-zammai" (Ocean-Reflection Samadhi), in *Master Dogen's Shobogenzo, Book* 2, trans. Gudo Nishijima and Chodo Cross (Dogen Sangha, 2006), 159.
2. From Dogen's *Shōbōgenzō*, "Fukanzazengi" (Universal Promotion of the Principles of Zazen), in *The Heart of Dōgen's Shōbōgenzō*, trans. Norman Waddell and Masao Abe (Albany: State University of New York Press, 2002), 4.
3. Taigen Dan Leighton, "Dogen's Zazen as Other-Power Practice," *Ancient Dragon Zen Gate*, February 18, 2019, https://www.ancientdragon.org/dogens-zazen-as-other-power-practice.

Chapter 17. Oneness of Self and Other

1. From Dogen's *Shōbōgenzō*, "Yuibutsu Yobutsu" (Only Buddha and Buddha), trans. Ed Brown and Kazuaki Tanahashi, in *Moon in a Dewdrop: Writings of Zen Master Dōgen*, ed. Kazuaki Tanahashi (New York: North Point Press, 1985), 162.
2. Martin Buber, *I and Thou*, trans. Walter Kaufmann (New York: Simon and Schuster, 1970), 59.

Chapter 18. Oneness and the Way of the Bodhisattva

1. Jacob Shamsian, "'I Wish I Could've Done More': A Woman Describes What It Was Like Trying to Help the Victims of the New Zealand Mosque Shooting," *Insider*, March 15, 2019, https://www.insider.com/new-zealand-mosque-shooting-woman-saving-victim-life-2019-3.
2. Dogen, "Caoshan's Dharmakāya," case no. 125, in *The True Dharma Eye: Zen Master Dōgen's Three Hundred Kōans*, trans. Kazuaki Tanahashi and John Daido Loori (Boulder, CO: Shambhala Publications, 2005), 170–71.
3. From Dogen's *Shōbōgenzō*, "Genjō Kōan" (Actualizing the Fundamental Point), trans. Robert Aitken and Kazuaki Tanahashi, in *Moon in a Dewdrop: Writings of Zen Master Dogen*, ed. Kazuaki Tanahashi (New York: North Point Press, 1985), 69.
4. From Dogen's *Shōbōgenzō*, "Bodaisatta-shishoho" (Four Virtues of the Bodhisattva), in *Eihei Dōgen: Mystical Realist*, trans. Hee-Jin Kim (Boston: Wisdom Publications, 2004), 211.

Chapter 19. Opening

1. From Dogen's *Shōbōgenzō*, "Uji" (The Time-Being), in *Eihei Dogen: Mystical Realist*, trans. Hee-Jin Kim (Boston: Wisdom Publications, 2004), 153.
2. Kodo Sawaki Roshi, "The Dharma Words of Homeless Kodo," *Shikantaza: An Introduction to Zazen*, trans. Shohaku Okumura (Kyoto: Kyoto Soto Zen Center, 1985), 119.
3. From Dogen's *Shōbōgenzō*, "Yuibutsu Yobutsu" (Only Buddha and Buddha), trans. Ed Brown and Kazuaki Tanahashi, in *Moon in a Dewdrop: Writings of Zen Master Dōgen*, ed. Kazuaki Tanahashi (New York: North Point Press, 1985), 162.
4. From Dogen's *Shōbōgenzō*, "Gyōbutsu-iigi" (Majestic Bearing of the Enactment-Buddha), in *Eihei Dōgen*, 72.
5. From Dogen's *Shōbōgenzō*, "Fukanzazengi" (Universal Promotion of the Principles of Zazen), in *The Heart of Dōgen's Shōbōgenzō*, trans. Norman Waddell and Masao Abe (Albany: State University of New York Press, 2002), 3.

Chapter 20. Oneness and Compassion

1. From Dogen's *Shōbōgenzō*, "Kenbutsu" (Meeting Buddha), in *Eihei Dogen: Mystical Realist*, trans. Hee-Jin Kim (Boston: Wisdom Publications, 2004), 208. Kim actually uses the word *thusness* where I use *suchness*, but I have opted to use the latter to keep continuity in the book.
2. From Dogen's *Shōbōgenzō*, "Yuibutsu Yobutsu" (Only Buddha and Buddha), translated by Ed Brown and Kazuaki Tanahashi, in *Moon in a Dewdrop: Writings of Zen Master Dōgen*, ed. Kazuaki Tanahashi (New York: North Point Press, 1985), 162.
3. From Dogen's *Shōbōgenzō*, "Sanjūshichihon Bodaibumpō" (Thirty-Seven Qualities of Enlightenment), in *Dōgen on Meditation and Thinking: A Reflection of His View of Zen*, trans. Hee-Jin Kim (Albany: State University of New York Press, 2007), 138n10.

Chapter 21. Oneness and the Precepts

1. Dogen, *Dōgen's Shōbōgenzō Zuimonki*, trans. Shohaku Okumura (Japan: Shotoshu Shumucho, 2018), 24.
2. Dogen, "Daigo" (Great Enlighenment), in *Dōgen on Meditation and Thinking: A Reflection on His View of Zen*, trans. Hee-Jin Kim (New York: State University of New York Press, 2007), 8.
3. From Dogen's *Shōbōgenzō*, "Gyobutsu-iigi," (Majestic Bearing of the Enactment-Buddha), in *Flowers of Emptiness*, trans. Hee-Jin Kim (Lewiston: The Edwin Mellen Press, 1985), 114.

Chapter 22. From *Not* to *Non*

1. From Dogen's *Shōbōgenzō*, "Immo" (Such), in *Classics of Buddhism and Zen, Volume* 2, trans. Thomas Cleary (Boston: Shambhala, 2005), 293.
2. From Dogen's *Shōbōgenzō*,"Immo" (Thusness), in *Flowers of Emptiness: Selections from Dogen's Shobogenzo*, trans. Hee-Jin Kim (Lewiston/Queenston: Edwin Mellen Press, 1985), 202.
3. Ludwig Wittgenstein, *Remarks on the Philosophy of Psychology*, vol. 2, trans. C. G. Luckhardt and M. A. E. Aue (Chicago: University of Chicago Press, 1980), no. 629.
4. From Dogen's *Shōbōgenzō*, "Gabyo" (The Pictured Cakes), in *Eihei Dogen: Mystical Realist*, trans. Hee-Jin Kim (Boston: Wisdom Publications, 2004), 66.

Chapter 24. Being a Buddha

1. From Dogen's *Shōbōgenzō*, "Shoho-jisso," (All things Themselves Are Their Ultimate Reality), in *Eihei Dogen: Mystical Realist*, trans. Hee-Jin Kim (Boston: Wisdom Publications, 2004), 204-5.
2. From Dogen's *Shōbōgenzō*, "Zuimonki" (Record of Things Heard), in *Eihei Dōgen: Mystical Realist*, trans. Hee-Jin Kim (Boston: Wisdom Publications, 2002), 69.
3. From Dogen's *Bendowa* (Talk on Wholehearted Practice of the Way), in *The Wholehearted Way: A Translation of Eihei Dogen's* Bendowa *with Commentary by Kōshō Uchiyama Roshi*, trans. Shohaku Okumura and Taigen Daniel Leighton (Rutland, VT: Tuttle Publishing, 1997), 19.
4. From Dogen's *Shōbōgenzō*, "Shoho-Jisso" (All things Themselves Are Their Ultimate Reality), in *Eihei Dogen*, 205.
5. From Dogen's *Shōbōgenzō*, "Sangai-yuishin" (The Triple World is Mind-Only), in *Eihei* Dogen, 123.
6. From Dogen's *Shōbōgenzō*, "Muchu-setsumu" (Expounding a Dream within a Dream), in *Eihei Dogen*, 243.
7. From Dogen's *Shōbōgenzō*, "Bussho" (Buddha-Nature), in *Eihei Dogen*, 126.
8. From Dogen's *Shōbōgenzō*, "Sanjūshichihon Bodaibumpo" (Thirty-seven Qualities of Enlightenment), in *Eihei Dogen*, 29.
9. Mechthild von Magdeburg, *Mystische Zeugnisse aller Zeiten unde Voelker*, trans. Ellie Eich (Munich: Diederichs, 1993), 135.

Library of Congress Cataloging-in-Publication Data
Names: Baker, Nancy Mujo, author.
Title: Opening to oneness: a practical and philosophical guide
to the Zen precepts / Nancy Mujo Baker.
Description: Boulder: Shambhala, 2022.
Identifiers: LCCN 2022012272 | ISBN 9781611809398 (trade paperback)
Subjects: LCSH: Religious life—Zen Buddhism. | Buddhist precepts. |
Zen Buddhism—Discipline. | Buddhist ethics.
Classification: LCC BQ9286.B35 2022 | DDC 294.3/927—dc23/eng/20220315
LC record available at https://lccn.loc.gov/2022012272